CW00434665

Microsoft® Visual Web Developer® 2008 Express Edition

Eric Griffin

PUBLISHED BY
Microsoft Press
A Division of Microsoft Corporation
One Microsoft Way
Redmond, Washington 98052-6399

Library of Congress Control Number: 2008938211

Printed and bound in the United States of America.

1 2 3 4 5 6 7 8 9   QWT   3 2 1 0 9 8

Distributed in Canada by H.B. Fenn and Company Ltd.

A CIP catalogue record for this book is available from the British Library.

Microsoft Press books are available through booksellers and distributors worldwide. For further information about international editions, contact your local Microsoft Corporation office or contact Microsoft Press International directly at fax (425) 936-7329. Visit our Web site at www.microsoft.com/mspress. Send comments to mspinput@microsoft.com.

Acquisitions Editor: Ben Ryan
Developmental Editor: Devon Musgrave
Project Editor: Valerie Woolley
Editorial Production: nSight, Inc.
Technical Reviewer: Umesh Patel; Technical Review services provided by Content Master, a member of CM Group, Ltd.
Cover: Tom Draper Design

Body Part No. X15-18140

I would like to dedicate this book to my parents, Floyd and Nathalie Griffin, who become wiser every day.

I would also like to dedicate this to my wife, Susan, and my children, Jonathan, Jamal, Bakari, Zachary, and AnnaGail. They sacrificed some of our time together during the writing of this book.

—Eric Griffin

Table of Contents

What do you think of this book? We want to hear from you!

Microsoft is interested in hearing your feedback so we can continually improve our books and learning resources for you. To participate in a brief online survey, please visit:

www.microsoft.com/learning/booksurvey/

What do you think of this book? We want to hear from you!

Microsoft is interested in hearing your feedback so we can continually improve our books and learning resources for you. To participate in a brief online survey, please visit:

www.microsoft.com/learning/booksurvey/

Introduction

Visual Web Developer 2008 is a modern Integrated Development Environment (IDE) that makes it easier for developers to create pages that use Web services, controls, and data. With Visual Web Developer, you can use .NET Framework 3.5 SP1 as a platform to create Web pages with ASP.NET. Web controls in ASP.NET are powerful reusable components to build dynamic data-driven Web pages.

Web Services is the technology of Web 2.0. A Web service is an application programming interface (API) that uses open Internet standards. With Visual Web Developer, you can integrate and create Web services with little coding.

Databases are important to creating robust, data-driven Web sites. From within Visual Web Developer, you can create databases by using Microsoft SQL Server Express edition. With ASP.NET data controls, you can add, update, and delete information from your pages.

Who This Book Is For

This book is for beginning Web programmers who want to learn how to create state-of-the-art Web sites.

Finding Your Best Starting Point in This Book

This book is designed to help you build skills in a number of essential areas. You can use this book if you are new to programming or if you have already worked with Visual Web Developer. This book uses one central Web site project called Personal Portal that you can see built from beginning to end. You can still explore specific areas if you don't want to walk through from the beginning.

Are you interested in	Follow these steps
How ASP.NET pages work	1. Copy the aspx files from Chapter 3 to a location on your hard drive. 2. Open each file for each step in the examples in the chapter to follow along.
Setting up site security	1. Copy Chapter 4\PersonalPortal and WebSites\PersonalPortal to the respective folders on your Visual Studio 2008 folder of your hard drive. 2. Walk through the chapter instructions to set up site security and login controls.

Master pages	1. Copy Chapter 4\PersonalPortal and WebSites\PersonalPortal to the respective folders on your Visual Studio 2008 folder of your hard drive.
	2. Walk through the chapter instructions to see how Master Pages can make a complex layout easy to create. Compare with the finished project located in Chapter 5\PersonalPortal WebSites\ PersonalPortal.
Server controls	1. Copy Chapter 5\PersonalPortal and WebSites\PersonalPortal to the respective folders on your Visual Studio 2008 folder of your hard drive.
	2. Walk through the chapter instructions. Compare with the finished project located in Chapter 6\PersonalPortal
Creating databases & ASP. NET data controls	1. Copy Chapter 7\PersonalPortal and WebSites\PersonalPortal to the respective folders on your Visual Studio 2008 folder of your hard drive.
	2. Walk through the chapter instructions. Compare with the finished project located in Chapter 8\PersonalPortal.

Conventions and Features in This Book

This book presents information using conventions designed to make the information readable and easy to follow. Before you start, read the following list, which explains conventions you'll see throughout the book and points out helpful features that you might want to use.

Conventions

- Each exercise is a series of tasks. Each task is presented as a series of numbered steps (1, 2, and so on). A round bullet (•) indicates an exercise that has only one step.

- Notes labeled "tip" provide additional information or alternative methods for completing a step successfully.

- Notes labeled "important" alert you to information you need to check before continuing.

- Text that you type appears in bold.

- A plus sign (+) between two key names means that you must press those keys at the same time. For example, "Press Alt+Tab" means that you hold down the Alt key while you press the Tab key.

Other Features

Sidebars throughout the book provide more in-depth information about the exercise. The sidebars might contain background information, design tips, or features related to the information being discussed.

Hardware and Software Requirements

You'll need the following hardware and software to complete the practice exercises in this book:

- Windows Vista Home Premium edition, Windows Vista Business edition, or Windows Vista Ultimate edition
- Microsoft Visual Web Developer 2008 Express edition SP1
- Microsoft SQL Server 2005 Express edition, Service Pack 2
- 2.4 GHz Pentium IV+ processor or faster
- 2 GB of available, physical RAM
- Video (800 ×600 or higher resolution) monitor with at least 256 colors
- CD-ROM or DVD-ROM drive
- Microsoft mouse or compatible pointing device

You will also need to have administrator access to your computer to configure SQL Server 2005 Express edition.

Code Samples

The companion CD inside this book contains the code samples that you'll use as you perform the exercises. By using the code samples, you won't waste time creating files that aren't relevant to the exercise. The files and the step-by-step instructions in the lessons also help you learn by doing, which is an easy and effective way to acquire and remember new skills.

Installing the Code Samples

Follow these steps to install the code samples and required software on your computer so that you can use them with the exercises.

1. Remove the companion CD from the package inside this book and insert it into your CD-ROM drive.

Note An end-user license agreement should open automatically. If this agreement does not appear, open **My Computer** on the desktop or **Start** menu, double-click the icon for your CD-ROM drive, and then double-click **StartCD.exe**.

2. Review the end-user license agreement. If you accept the terms, select the accept option and then click **Next**.

A menu will appear with options related to the book.

3. Click **Install Code Samples**.

4. Follow the instructions that appear.

The code samples are installed in the following location on your computer:

Documents\Microsoft Press\VisWebDev Step By Step

Using the Code Samples

Each chapter in this book explains when and how to use any code samples for that chapter. When it's time to use a code sample, the book will list the instructions for how to open the files.

For those of you who like to know all the details, here's a list of the code sample Visual Studio 2008 projects and solutions, grouped by the folders where you can find them.

Project	Description
Chapter 3	
Default.aspx Default[a-f].aspx	Follow along with the book with versions of the Default.aspx page starting with Defaulta.aspx through Defaultf.aspx.
Chapter 4	
Blank Site Security and Login	In this chapter, you begin to work on the personal portal. You learn how to set up your site security and add new users. Looking under the hood, you discover where ASP.NET stores its security data. Using the ASP.NET built-in Login server controls, you add a Login page and a way for users to log out and change their password.
Chapter 5	
PersonalPortal WebSites/PersonalPortal	In this chapter, you learn how to use master pages to create reusable markup and provide a consistent look and feel for your site.
Chapter 6	
PersonalPortal WebSites/PersonalPortal	In this chapter, you learn how to use a few of the dozens of server controls available to you in Visual Web Developer and ASP.NET.

Chapter 7

PersonalPortal
WebSites/PersonalPortal

In this chapter, you learn how to integrate the Virtual Earth map control into the personal portal. You use JavaScript and HTML in the Visual Web Developer editor to do this. You also learn how to debug JavaScript. While debugging, you learn how to inspect JavaScript variable values and change them on the fly.

Chapter 8

PersonalPortal
WebSites/PersonalPortal

In this chapter, you learn how to create a database. You learn that databases consist of one or more tables. These tables are structured with columns of a specific type to constrain the values stored within it. These columns are used to make rows of values for the user or application to fill in.

Chapter 9

PersonalPortal
WebSites/PersonalPortal

In this chapter, you learn how to create a data-driven user interface for to-dos in the personal portal. You learn how to create a *DataSet* and corresponding data tables to represent the *ToDo* database. You create queries in table adapters to retrieve and update data. You learn how to use *GridView* to display and edit to-dos and how to add new to-dos by using *DetailsView*.

Chapter 10

PersonalPortal
WebSites/PersonalPortal

In this chapter, you learn about cascading style sheets (CSS). You learn how to attach an existing style sheet to an ASP.NET page. You learn how to find the definition of styles and how to apply the style to an element. You style the personal portal by using a style sheet to display a banner and section headers with an image. You also style the data interface controls.

Chapter 11

PersonalPortal
WebSites/PersonalPortal

In this chapter, you learn about mashups. Mashups are small programs that integrate APIs and data from different and sometimes competing companies. Microsoft Popfly is the new mashup creation software by which you create mashups quickly and without coding. Popfly Explorer, a Visual Web Developer add-in, enables you to embed mashups within ASP.NET pages.

Chapter 12

PersonalPortal
WebSites/PersonalPortal

In this chapter, you learn about Web services. You learn how to upload documents to the server and create your own Web service, reference it in a project, and then use it in an ASP.NET page.

Chapter 13

PersonalPortal
Websites/PersonalPortal

In this last chapter, you explore how you can transfer your personal portal project to a remote Web server. You simulate this by installing a Web server, called Microsoft Internet Information Server, on your PC; this comes built into Windows Vista. You then use the Copy Web Site feature in Visual Web Developer to transfer the entire site with a button click.

Uninstalling the Code Samples

Follow these steps to remove the code samples from your computer.

1. In **Control Panel**, open **Add Or Remove Programs**.

2. From the **Currently Installed Programs** list, select **<VisWebDev Step by Step>**.

3. Click **Remove**.

4. Follow the instructions to remove the code samples.

> **Find Additional Content Online** As new or updated material becomes available that complements your book, it will be posted online on the Microsoft Press Online Developer Tools Web site. The type of material you might find includes updates to book content, articles, links to companion content, errata, sample chapters, and more. This Web site is available at *http://www.microsoft.com/learning/books/online/developer* and is updated periodically.

Support for This Book

Every effort has been made to ensure the accuracy of this book and the contents of the companion CD. As corrections or changes are collected, they will be added to a Microsoft Knowledge Base article.

Microsoft Press provides support for books and companion CDs at the following Web site: *http://www.microsoft.com/learning/support/books/.*

> **Digital Content for Digital Book Readers:** If you bought a digital-only edition of this book, you can enjoy select content from the print edition's companion CD.
> Visit *http://go.microsoft.com/fwlink/?LinkId=130772* to get your downloadable content. This content is always up-to-date and available to all readers.

Questions and Comments

If you have comments, questions, or ideas regarding the book or the companion CD or questions that are not answered by visiting the sites mentioned, please send them to Microsoft Press by e-mail to: *mspinput@microsoft.com.*

Or by postal mail to:

Microsoft Press
Attn: *Microsoft Visual Web Developer 2008 Express Edition Step by Step* Editor
One Microsoft Way
Redmond, WA 98052-6399

Please note that Microsoft software product support is not offered through the preceding addresses.

Chapter 1
Introducing Visual Web Developer 2008

After completing this chapter, you will be able to

- Understand why Visual Web Developer is the best tool with which to build Web sites.

- Understand the difference between HTML and server controls.

- Understand HTML and how it relates to JavaScript.

- Understand what ASP.NET is and how it relates to C# and the .NET Framework.

- Understand how data is represented in databases and XML.

There can be many reasons you are reading this book. You might be an avid Internet user who wants to learn how to create the cool sites you've seen. You might be an Information Technology (IT) professional who wants learn a new skill. Or you might be a Web programmer who hasn't created a site in a while and wants to learn state-of-the-art Web development. No matter who you are, no matter what your reasons, you want to get up to speed fast. And you want to do it step by step.

I read hundreds of reviews of technical books on Web sites such as Amazon to figure out the best way to write this book. I discovered a common complaint. Many technical books give snippets or throw-away examples that don't fit into a larger solution. In each chapter, the reader is prompted to retrieve an example from a corresponding folder on an accompanying CD. After the user is finished with the chapter, the example is discarded. This results in a disjointed learning experience for the reader, who learns what the technology is capable of; however, applying knowledge of the technology to a problem is difficult because the lesson lacks a larger solution context.

Readers want a beginning-to-end learning experience. They want complete solutions that can help them figure out the when, where, and why of using the technology to solve problems.

This book will follow this principle. Starting in Chapter 4, "Creating Your First Web Site," I will introduce the concept of a *personal portal* Web site. From conception to deployment, I will step you through the process of creating your own personal site. Along the way, you will learn how to do some of the cool stuff such as embedding Virtual Earth maps and popfly mashups on a Web page, creating dynamic data-driven pages; uploading documents to the server; and holding into Web services.

Note You might not be familiar with buzzwords such as Virtual Earth and mashups. Don't worry; I will introduce you to them and show you where to learn more.

Why Visual Studio Web Developer

I want to reassure you that you have chosen the right tool for building modern Web sites. Also referred to as an Integrated Development Environment (IDE), Visual Web Developer 2008 makes it easier for developers to create pages that use Web services, controls, and data. Figure 1-1 shows Visual Web Developer as the central productivity tool that integrates these technologies.

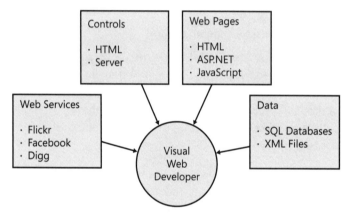

FIGURE 1-1 Visual Web Developer helps you build Web pages with data, controls, and Web services.

Web Pages

Web pages are what you see in the browser. They are also called HTML pages. However, as you have experienced on the Internet, Web sites are becoming richer and more interactive. The line is blurring between desktop applications such as Microsoft Outlook and Web sites. This new evolution of desktop-like Web sites is called Rich Internet Applications.

Clients and Servers

With the emergence of Rich Internet Applications, it's important to understand how things work between clients and servers. When you access a Web page on the Internet by typing a Universal Resource Locator (URL) such as *http://www.microsoft.com* in your browser (the client), you are sending a request by using a network protocol called Hypertext Transfer Protocol (HTTP) to the Microsoft Web site (the server). See Figure 1-2.

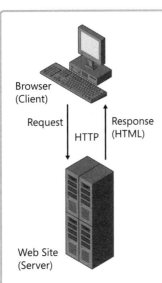

FIGURE 1-2 Communication between a browser (the client) and a Web site (the server).

In response, the server returns information to the browser to display. The format of that information is a Web page in Hypertext Markup Language (HTML). All browsers display HTML.

HTML

At the heart of most Web pages is HTML. HTML is text that is marked up in a standard format so that browsers can display an interface. Here is a simple Web page that you can type in Notepad, save as a file with an .html extension, and then open in your browser.

LISTING 1-1 Simple HTML Page

```
<html>
    Hello World!
</html>
```

The <html> in the preceding listing is called a tag. A tag is enclosed in angle brackets: < >. A tag encloses text or other tags with a leading <tag> and closing </tag>.

LISTING 1-2 Simple HTML Page with Bold Text

```
<html>
    <b>Hello World!</b>
</html>
```

By enclosing the Hello World! text in a <b> tag, the browser displays the text in bold.

HTML has evolved over the years and has become more complicated since its introduction in 1993. If you want to see more complicated HTML, view the source HTML of your favorite Web site. You can do it from any browser. From Microsoft Internet Explorer:

1. Open Internet Explorer to a Web site such as *http://www.msn.com*.

2. Select Source from the View menu.

As you can see by examining the source, HTML can get very complicated; the large amount of HTML required to display a Web page can be overwhelming.

For many years, complicated pages within sites like MSN.com were created with text editors. They were hand typed with nothing more than an application such as Notepad. Visual Web Developer has an advanced editor with many shortcuts and time savers for developers writing HTML. We will explore them further in Chapter 3, "Creating Your First ASP.NET Page."

JavaScript

JavaScript, first deployed in Netscape Navigator 2.0 in 1995, has been adopted as the Internet standard for client programmability. It is within all major browsers. If you are familiar with C or C++, you will find similarities in JavaScript. As mentioned earlier, it is on the client as opposed to the server, which means it cannot directly manipulate components on the server. That doesn't mean it cannot communicate with server components. Because HTML has tags for JavaScript, you can embed custom functionality in Web pages. This functionality operates within the confines of the browser only. Here is a simple JavaScript function embedded in your simple HTML page.

LISTING 1-3 Simple HTML Page with JavaScript

```
<html>
    <script type="text/javascript" language="javascript">
function SayHello()
{
    alert("Hello World!");
}
    </script>
        <input id="SayHelloButton" type="button" value="button" onclick="SayHello();"/>
</html>
```

An HTML input of type **button** with an *id* attribute of *SayHelloButton* fires off a JavaScript statement that calls the *SayHello()* function. It displays a dialog box that states "Hello World!" In Visual Web Developer 2008, JavaScript is fully supported in the editor with shortcuts and the new functionality of JavaScript debugging. I will cover more about debugging, what it is, and how to do it, in Chapter 7, "Working with HTML and JavaScript."

ASP.NET 3.5

Active Server Pages (ASP) and .NET were designed to make the daunting task of creating dynamic, interactive, data-driven Web pages easy. First introduced as ASP.NET 1.0 in 2002, ASP.NET has, like HTML, evolved to version 3.5 to keep up with the demands of the Internet. It is a server-based technology. In many ways, which we will explore in this book, ASP.NET simplifies the development of pages and generates hundreds of lines of HTML on the fly for you.

> **Note** ASP.NET is a rich technology by which you can build your Web sites. Although this book will cover many aspects of ASP.NET, covering ASP.NET architecture is beyond the scope of this book. A great reference is *ASP.NET 3.5 Step by Step* by George Shepherd (Microsoft Press, 2008). I will refer to it throughout this book for you to get a deeper understanding.

The ".NET" in ASP.NET refers to the Microsoft .NET Framework. Also introduced in 2002, it is the foundation of ASP. Within the .NET Framework are reusable components called classes. These classes contain functionality that you can access using C# (pronounced "see-sharp"). For those of you familiar with C or C++ or even JavaScript, C# should look very familiar. It is a rich, powerful, and expressive language for building programming logic or your own reusable components.

> **Note** An in-depth look into C# is beyond the scope of this book. A good reference for deeper understanding is *Visual C# Step by Step 2008* by John Sharp (Microsoft Press, 2008).

Visual Web Developer was designed to build ASP.NET pages with any .NET language, such as C#. As with HTML, the editor in Visual Web Developer is tightly integrated with the .NET platform and provides many as-you-type productivity features that you will explore starting in Chapter 3.

Controls

One specialized type of reusable component is controls. Often visual, they enable a developer to add functionality to pages quickly. Controls are things such as buttons and text boxes that you place on Web pages.

HTML Controls

If you look at Listing 1-3, "Simple HTML Page with JavaScript," shown earlier, you will notice the <input> tag. This tag tells the browser, along with the *type* attribute set to a value of *button*, to create a button control on the Web page.

LISTING 1-4 An HTML Control

```
<input id="SayHelloButton" type="button" value="Say Hello" onclick="SayHello();"/>
```

> **Note** Attributes are additional bits of information that can be added within a tag to define the tag further. The attributes for the HTML control shown are *id*, *type*, and *onclick*.

HTML pages fire events on the browser to create interactivity. The *onclick* attribute in the <input> tag is an event fired by the HTML page when a user clicks the button. The JavaScript statement assigned as the *onclick* value is executed.

Server Controls

Introduced with ASP.NET, server controls look like HTML controls. The power in server controls is that the code is executed on the server. This means you are not limited to using JavaScript to create interactivity. You can use any language supported by .NET, including C#. Following is a server control that is similar to the HTML control I showed you earlier.

LISTING 1-5 A Server Control

```
<asp:Button id="Button1" runat="server" text="Say Hello" onclick="Button1_Click1" />
```

The server control is defined by a tag, but it is prefixed with asp:. This prefix denotes the tag as an ASP.NET tag and is processed differently when the server returns HTML to the client.

Let's compare the HTML and server controls:

- Instead of being indicated as an <input> tag and a type attribute assigning the type of input as a button, asp:Button is used.

- The *id* attribute is the same.

- However, a *runat* attribute is set to *"server"* to indicate that this is a server control that will execute on the server.

- The *text* attribute is used instead of the *value* attribute to set the button's display name.

- The *onclick* is the same, but the big difference is that the function being called is actually a C# class with a method (a special type of function) called *Button1_Click1*.

Data

Everything in Web development begins and ends with data. Without it, the Web has no meaning. The value of a Web site is directly related to the data it stores. Some data is created for the user, and some data is added by the user. Flickr (*http://www.flickr.com*), a photo storage Web site, is a great example of value being created by users adding their own data (their pictures). Now you can search millions of interesting photos from Flickr's data store.

Databases

Databases are a standard way of storing data. A variety of vendors such as Microsoft, Oracle, and IBM provide proprietary database products that are optimized to store and retrieve data quickly. Databases further group data into tables that can be related to each other.

The downside to databases is that their formats are not compatible with each other and are not human readable. All vendors do support a data retrieval language called Structured Query Language (SQL). SQL is used to retrieve and relate information from tables for consumption by languages such as C#. Visual Web Developer has features called designers to help you work with databases and build queries for your pages. You will learn more about creating and using databases in Chapter 8, "Working with Databases," and Chapter 9, "Building Data-Driven User Interfaces."

XML

Extensible Markup Language (XML), initially defined in 1998, has become a new standard for storing data. Readable by humans and defined in text, XML is easy to create.

LISTING 1-6 Simple XML

```
<food>
 <desert>Cake</desert>
 <desert>Ice Cream</desert>
</food>
```

If you think the preceding example looks like HTML, you are correct. HTML uses tags to denote pages, and XML uses tags to denote data elements. You will use XML in the solution you create in this book.

Web Services

Web services is a new way to communicate with servers that is richer and more open than the simple request and response between a browser and Web site. Instead of returning HTML to the client from the server, XML is used to send data. Adopted by most industry leaders such as Microsoft, Yahoo!, and Google, and Web sites such as Flickr, Facebook, and Digg, Web services is the new way vendors are exposing application programming interfaces (APIs) to their products and services.

The built-in tools of Visual Web Developer allow you to discover, integrate, and consume Web services from different vendors seamlessly. You will learn more about that in Chapter 12, "Working with Web Services."

Summary

In this chapter, you have learned how Visual Web Developer enables you to create rich Web pages that integrate data, controls, and Web services. You have learned the relationship between clients and servers. In Chapter 2, "Working in Visual Web Developer 2008," you will install Visual Web Developer and learn more about its menus and windows and how to use integrated help.

Chapter 2
Working in Visual Web Developer 2008

After completing this chapter, you will be able to

- Install Visual Web Developer 2008.

- Use Start Page.

- Dock and auto-hide windows.

- Hide, unhide, and customize toolbars.

- Find the relevant folders Visual Web Developer uses.

In this chapter, you install Visual Web Developer and walk through its interface. You can download the installation file by visiting the Visual Web Developer home page at *http://www. microsoft.com/express/vwd*. (See Figure 2-1.)

FIGURE 2-1 Visual Web Developer home page.

To download the installation file

1. Click the **Download Now** link. The Downloads page displays. Select the language from the Visual Web Developer section of the page and click the **Download** link.

2. You will be prompted with a file download dialog box for the installation file called vnssetup.exe. (See Figure 2-2.)

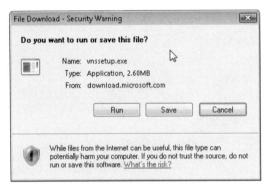

FIGURE 2-2 File download dialog box.

3. Click **Save** to download **vnssetup.exe** to a directory on your computer such as the Downloads folder (Windows Vista only). After completing the download, navigate to the **Downloads** folder.

> **Note** Notice that vnssetup.exe is only 2.6 MB. This application begins only the installation process. As you will see during the installation process, hundreds more megabytes have to be downloaded.

You need administrator privileges on your computer to install Visual Web Developer. In Windows Vista, right-click **vnssetup.exe** and choose **Run As Administrator**.

Figure 2-3 shows the first dialog box you see.

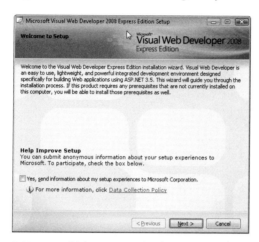

FIGURE 2-3 Welcome To Setup dialog box.

4. Click the **Next** button after you select the **Yes, send information about my setup experiences to Microsoft Corporation** check box.

5. The next dialog box to appear is shown in Figure 2-4. Accept the terms of the license agreement (do read the license agreement) and leave the Allow Visual Studio To Display Online RSS Content On The Start Page selected (more about this later in the chapter). Click the **Next** button.

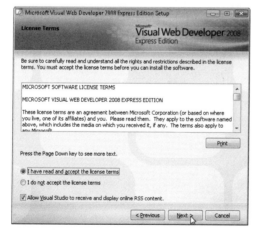

FIGURE 2-4 Accept license terms.

6. Select all three options in the next dialog box and click **Next**. (See Figure 2-5.)

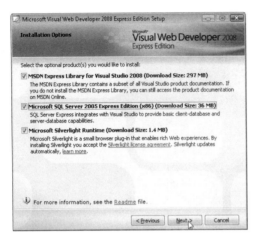

FIGURE 2-5 Install other options.

7. Decide whether you want to keep C:\Program Files\Microsoft Visual Studio 9.0\ as the destination folder. (See Figure 2-6.) Visual Web Developer functions the same if you choose a different directory. Click **Install** to begin the installation. Remember to ensure an active Internet connection before starting.

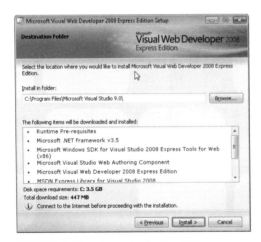

FIGURE 2-6 Choosing a destination folder.

A new installation progress dialog box appears. (See Figure 2-7.) Each of the nine components will be downloaded first, before installation. This might take some minutes, depending on your Internet connection speed. Remember, the MSDN library alone is 297 MB. Right now would be a good time for a coffee break.

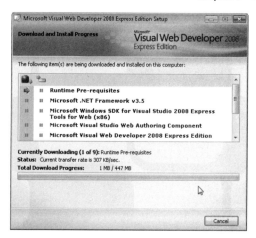

FIGURE 2-7 Download And Install Progress dialog box.

Keep checking back on the installation to make sure everything is moving along. Some components might require you to restart your computer. If a reboot is necessary, the installation will prompt you for the username and password if it is required. The installation time, depending on your Internet connection speed, could take almost an hour to complete.

After the installation has completed successfully, you will be presented with a Setup Complete dialog box. (See Figure 2-8.)

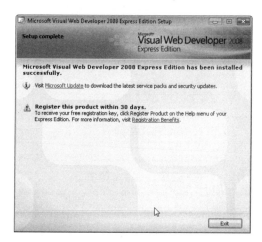

FIGURE 2-8 Setup Complete dialog box.

8. Follow the advice in the dialog box and run Microsoft Update by clicking the link to ensure that you have the latest updates for Visual Web Developer.

You don't have to worry about registering Visual Web Developer immediately. You have 30 days, but the registration process is fast and straightforward so I recommend getting it out of the way. After all, Visual Web Developer is free.

Running Visual Web Developer for the First Time

Now that you have installed Visual Web Developer, you can start it by clicking the **Visual Web Developer 2008 Express Edition** icon found on your start menu. The first time, Visual Web Developer starts the dialog box displayed in Figure 2-9.

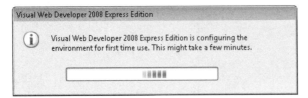

FIGURE 2-9 Setup Complete dialog box.

After a few minutes, the Visual Web Developer interface displays as shown in Figure 2-10.

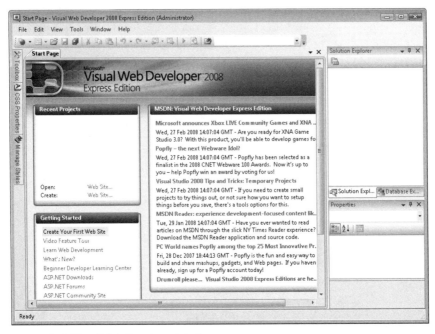

FIGURE 2-10 Visual Web Developer interface.

Figure 2-10 shows the eight windows that are open by default when you start Visual Web Developer. They are the Toolbox, CCS Properties, and Manage Styles windows docked and auto-hidden vertically to the left. Start Page is in the center. Solution Explorer and Database Explorer are docked to the right and on top of the docked Properties windows to the lower right.

You will find out more about the functionality of each window, starting in Chapter 4, "Creating Your First Web Site," except for Start Page. I will also explain how docking and auto-hiding work.

Start Page

Referring to Figure 2-10, at the center of the Visual Web Developer is Start Page. It's divided into three main sections. The Recent Projects section in the upper left of the page shows the recent projects you have created. Because you haven't created anything yet, you don't see anything here. You will start doing that in Chapter 4. The Getting Started section contains videos, tutorials, and Web sites with training and documentation on how to use Visual Web Developer. Below it (and not showing in Figure 2-10) are the Visual Web Developer headlines. This section displays a list of links to the latest news articles about Visual Web Developer. The MSDN "Visual Web Developer Express Edition" section displays an RSS feed from the MSDN Web site. This is updated every time you open Visual Web Developer.

Clicking any of the links opens the Visual Web Developer built-in browser. A new tab will display with the contents of the link. You can close the tab by clicking the X in the upper right corner of Start Page.

Working with Visual Web Developer Windows

Using the Visual Web Developer windows is a fundamental skill that you must understand while developing Web sites. Let's start by understanding how to move, dock, and auto-hide windows.

With Visual Web Developer open:

1. Click the Properties window and drag the window to the left and center of Visual Web Developer. (Eight icons with arrows should appear, as shown in Figure 2-11.)

2. Drag the window over the center top icon with the arrow pointing up.

   You should see the icon highlight and a transparent highlight will appear over the top half of Start Page.

3. Release the mouse when the icon highlights.

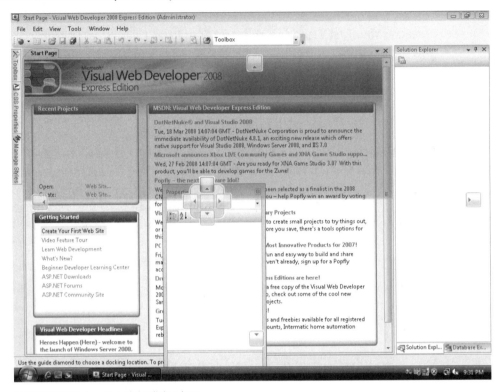

FIGURE 2-11 Setup complete dialog box.

The Properties window will dock on top of **Start Page**. It will stay in that location until you close it, auto-hide it, or move it. Let's auto-hide it to see what happens.

To auto-hide the Properties window, click the pushpin icon pointing down in the upper right of the Properties window. (See Figure 2-12.)

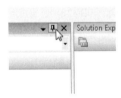

FIGURE 2-12 Auto-hiding the Properties window.

Auto-hiding the Properties window minimizes it so it will look like Figure 2-13. Notice that the minimized window location is at the top of the Visual Web Developer, where you docked it. Windows will minimize where you dock them. In the present case, the Toolbox, CSS Properties, and Manage Styles windows are docked and auto-hidden to the left of Visual Web Developer.

Clicking the Properties window while it is auto-hiding displays the entire window. If you click or move the mouse focus to another window in Visual Web Developer, the window will minimize again.

FIGURE 2-13 Minimized Properties window.

To move the Properties window back to its original location

1. Click the Properties window while it's minimized.

2. First, expand it by clicking the pushpin (now pointing to the left).

   This causes the window to return to its original size.

3. Click the top of the window and drag it to the lower right of Visual Web Developer.

   The icons with arrows should appear, but when you move the Properties window to the far right, the icons will move to the right of Visual Web Developer. (See Figure 2-14.)

4. Hover the window over the bottom arrow pointing down until the arrow highlights.

   You should see the region below Solution Explorer highlight.

5. Release the mouse. The Properties window should return to its original location.

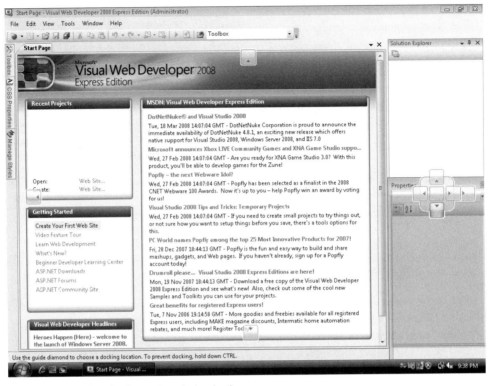

FIGURE 2-14 Moving the Properties window back.

You can practice with the rest of the windows as much as you want. If you ever get into trouble and want to return the windows to the original settings, select **Reset Window Layout** from the **Windows** menu to retrieve the original windows and their placements.

Working with Visual Web Developer Menus

Now is a good time to talk about Visual Web Developer menus. Visual Web Developer has six menus: File, Edit, View, Tools, Window, and Help. As you read this book, you will become familiar with these menus. I won't go into detail about each of them.

File

The File menu is similar to other applications you have used. It is where you open files, Web sites, and Visual Web Developer projects and create new files.

Edit

The Edit menu should also be familiar. It has the standard Undo, Cut, Copy, Paste, Find, and Replace menu items. You will use these menus extensively when you are editing code in the Visual Web Developer editor.

View

The View menu contains all the menu items for the specialized windows within Visual Web Developer, including the Properties, Toolbox, and Solution Explorer windows, to name a few. Selecting any of these menu items opens the corresponding window.

Tools

The Tools menu has menu items you use to customize your Visual Web Developer experience. You can manage external tools and add reusable components to speed your development.

Window

The Window menu helps you organize the windows in Visual Web Developer. As you develop, you need to look at several windows. This can get confusing very quickly. Understanding how to retain control of all the windows is essential to efficiency.

Help

Help is another essential menu. It is your conduit into the extensive MSDN documentation you installed locally and MSDN documentation online (*http://msdn.microsoft.com*).

Working with Visual Web Developer Toolbars

Like many applications, Visual Web Developer gives you keyboard shortcuts to commonly used menu items and toolbars. Visual Web Developer has more than 15 toolbars—Formatting, Debugging, HTML Source Editing, and Style Sheets, to name a few. By default, all the toolbars except the standard toolbar are hidden. To expose the remaining toolbars, right-click the standard toolbar.

A drop-down menu displays the hidden toolbars. (See Figure 2-15.) Selecting the toolbar inserts a check before it on the menu and makes it visible. Selecting a checked-marked toolbar hides it.

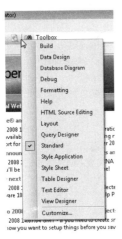

FIGURE 2-15 Displaying the available toolbars.

In addition to being able to hide or expose toolbars, you can customize all the toolbars to give you flexibility in which commands you want on a toolbar.

Selecting **Customize** from the drop-down window shows the selected toolbar to hide it if desired. (See Figure 2-16.)

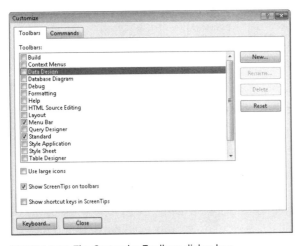

FIGURE 2-16 The Customize Toolbars dialog box.

Toolbar Dialog Box

On the Toolbars tab, you can select and cancel toolbars you want visible or hidden. You can also, optionally, select whether you want to use larger icons on the toolbar, show tooltips, or show keyboard shortcuts in the toolbars.

You can also create a new custom toolbar by clicking the **New** button. If you created a custom menu, you can rename it by selecting it in the **Toolbars** list and clicking **Rename**. You can delete it by clicking **Delete**. If you feel you have created a mess and want to restore a toolbar, you can click **Reset**.

The **Commands** tab enables you to rearrange the order of the commands on the toolbars and on the menus. You can drag and drop the command onto the Visual Web Developer toolbar, if the toolbar is visible, to set its exact location. If you make some mistakes, go back to **Reset**.

Understanding Visual Studio Web Developer Folders

A lot happened during the installation of Visual Web Developer. Let's examine the folders you will be using when you use Visual Web Developer. You should already know one directory that was created. You selected it as the primary installation location for Visual Web Developer. If you used the default location, it is C:\Program Files\Microsoft Visual Studio 9.0\. You will find folders containing installation files and the components necessary to run Visual Web Developer in this directory. However, this directory is not the one in which you will spend most of your time. If you go to your Documents folder in Windows Vista or your My Documents folder in Windows XP, you will find a folder called Visual Studio 2008. Here you will find folders called Code Snippets, Projects, Settings, Templates, Visualizers, and WebSites.

The Code Snippets folder stores small pieces of code you might want to reuse. The Projects folder stores the settings for your creations, using Visual Web Developer, called projects and solutions. The Settings folder stores customizations and preferences, such as window and toolbar changes, you configure while using Visual Web Developer. The Templates folder stores reusable customizations and preferences on a project or solution level. Visualizers are used during the debugging process. This book won't be covering Visualizers, but this is where they are located and installed. You can probably figure out that the WebSites folder is where Web sites you create are located. It is used in combination with the Projects folder.

As you walk through the creation of the sample site, you will revisit these folders to see how the contents change.

Summary

In this chapter, you learned how to install Visual Studio Web Developer. You learned how to dock and auto-hide its windows. You learned how to hide, expose, and customize toolbars. You've also learned about the folders Visual Web Developer uses. Now that you are familiar with Visual Web Developer, you will create your first ASP.NET page in Chapter 3, "Creating Your First ASP.NET Page."

Chapter 3
Creating Your First ASP.NET Page

After completing this chapter, you will be able to

- Designate where and how client and server code execute.

- Understand how JavaScript and C# work on a page.

- Add HTML to pages dynamically, using JavaScript's *Document* object.

- Add HTML to pages dynamically, using the ASP.NET *Response* object.

- Pass parameters in URLs and process them using the ASP.NET *Request* object.

- Create client controls for use with JavaScript.

- Create server controls for use with ASP.NET.

In this chapter, you learn how to create your first ASP.NET page. It is very important to understand what is happening at a basic level. You explore all the fundamental functionality in ASP.NET pages. In Chapter 4, "Creating Your First Web Site," you start the personal portal that you will build from beginning to end.

In Chapter 1, "Introducing Visual Web Developer 2008," I talked about client and server computing. You learned that the client is your personal computer, and the browser is a specialized application that requests information from the server. The server also has an application that responds to the client. It is called a Web server.

A Web server is a specialized application that communicates with clients by using Hypertext Transfer Protocol (HTTP). Web servers handle all the incoming HTTP requests for you and host the Web pages of the Web site. As hosts, Web servers are extended with application programming interfaces (APIs) to facilitate building Web sites. ASP.NET is the extending API on Microsoft Windows Server 2003 and its Internet Information Server (IIS) Web server, through which you can use .NET Framework languages such as Microsoft Visual Basic C# to create dynamic, data-driven Web sites.

Don't worry; you don't have to have a computer running Windows Server 2003 to develop Web sites with Visual Web Developer. It has its own built-in Web server (extended with ASP.NET) that can run on Microsoft Windows XP and Windows Vista.

Note If you are looking for a deep understanding of the API and architecture of ASP.NET, see *Microsoft ASP.NET 3.5 Step by Step* by George Shepherd (Microsoft Press, 2008).

Creating an ASP.NET Web Form

You will not create a Web site until Chapter 4. Web sites are more complicated, so for now, keep things simple; just create a single, standalone Web page.

To create your first ASP.NET page in Visual Web Developer

1. Open Visual Web Developer.

2. From the **File** menu, select **New File**.

   The dialog box illustrated in Figure 3-1 appears.

3. Select **Web** from the Categories list to expand it and select **C#**.

   There are 15 Microsoft Visual Studio installed templates for you to choose from. I will touch on many of these templates in this book. For now, you just create a **Web form**.

4. Select **Web Form** and click **Open**.

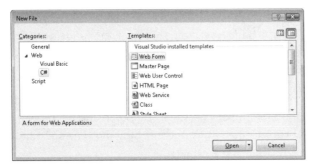

FIGURE 3-1 New file dialog box.

The Visual Web Developer editor opens in front of Start Page and displays the code shown in Listing 3-1. This is a Web form.

LISTING 3-1 An Empty Web Form Template

```
<%@ Page Language="C#" %>
<!DOCTYPE html PUBLIC "-//W3C//DTD XHTML 1.0 Transitional//EN" "http://www.w3.org/TR/xhtml1/
DTD/xhtml1-transitional.dtd">

<script runat="server">

</script>

<html xmlns="http://www.w3.org/1999/xhtml">

<head runat="server">
<title>Untitled Page</title>
  </head>
    <body>
```

```
   <form id="form1" runat="server">

    <div>

    </div>

    </form>

  </body>
</html>
```

Let's go line by line. The first line, <%@ Page Language="C#" %>, is markup code ASP.NET uses to indicate that this is an ASP.NET page and to determine which language (in this case, C#) will be used by the server-side code. (I'll talk more about this later.)

The second line is markup to designate compliance with the Extensible Hypertext Markup Language (XHTML) standard and its validation file, called a Document Type Definition (DTD). This appears on every page; it's used by browsers and shouldn't be touched.

The <script/> tag is empty by default, with an attribute called *runat* with a value of *server*. As you learn later in this chapter, this is where C# code can execute on the server.

The next tag, <html>, you should recognize. You don't have a Web page if you don't have the <html> tag. It has a standard, don't-touch attribute called *xmlns* that tells the browser to interpret the Hypertext Markup Language (HTML) according to the XHTML standard.

The <head> tag is also a standard HTML tag, with an enclosed <title> tag to name the page (Untitled Page). It also has a *runat* attribute. Enclosed in the standard HTML <body> tag is a standard <form> tag with an *id* attribute of *form1* and a *runat* attribute set to *server*. Inside it is a standard <div> tag.

Previewing a Web Form in a Browser

Now that you have walked through the markup, let's see what it will look like in a browser. Before you do that, save the page.

Save a new Web form

1. From the **File** menu, click **Save Default1.aspx**.

   All ASP.NET pages have the .aspx extension.

 Note Visual Web Developer automatically suggests a name for you. "Default" is a typical name for a Web page.

   Visual Web Developer will open a Save File As dialog box, as you see in Figure 3-2.

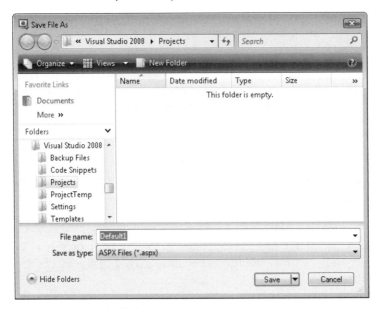

FIGURE 3-2 Saving the Default.aspx page.

2. Open your **Documents** folder in Windows Vista or your **My Documents** folder in Windows XP and find the Visual Studio 2008 directory that was created during installation.

3. Save the file in the **Projects** folder as **Default1.aspx**.

Now that you have saved the file, you can preview it in a Web browser.

Previewing the Web form in a Web browser

1. From the **File** menu, select **View in Browser** or click the **View in Browser** icon on the standard toolbar.

FIGURE 3-3 View In Browser icon.

2. Your default browser appears. See Figure 3-4.

   At the time of writing, I am using a Preview version of Microsoft Internet Explorer 8.

This first thing you notice is the URL. On my computer, it is *http://localhost:49584/Project/ Default1.aspx*. What does this mean? It means that you are running the ASP.NET page from the Projects folder on your computer. *Localhost* is a standard naming convention for Web servers running locally on a computer. The number 49584 is the port number the Web server uses to communicate, using HTTP with the browser.

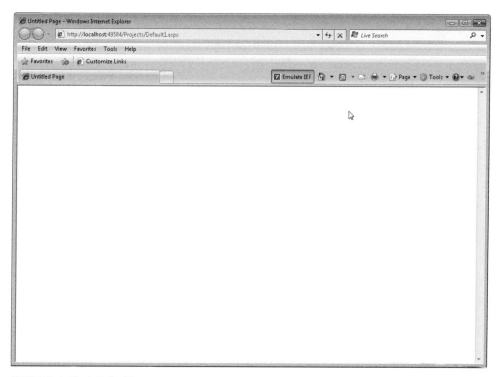

FIGURE 3-4 Blank Default1.aspx page.

The second thing you might notice is an icon in the lower half of your computer screen. In Windows Vista and Windows XP, an icon similar to the View In Browser icon you clicked on the toolbar appears. Double-click the icon to open the dialog box shown in Figure 3-5.

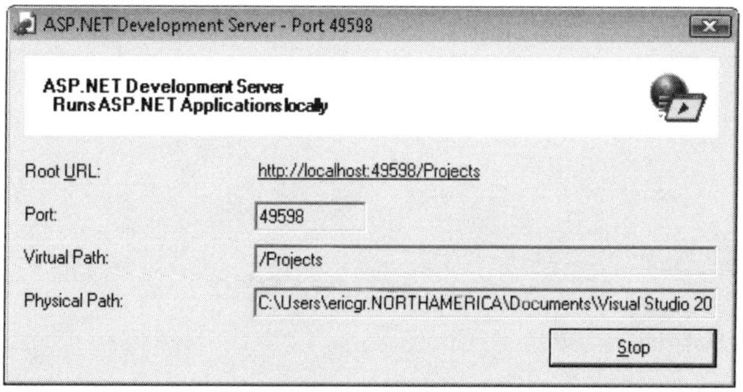

FIGURE 3-5 ASP.NET Development Server window.

It is the Visual Web Developer built-in Web server called ASP.NET Development Server. It has details about the root URL, port, virtual path, and physical location of the Web page you are running. If you click the **Stop** button, the Web server will shut down and be removed from memory. You don't want to do this yet.

> **Note** There is a lot more to Web servers, but you don't have to understand it deeply. Visual Web Developer handles all the setup for you. You will learn more about Web servers, how they work, and how to configure them in later chapters.

Close the ASP.NET Development Server window and return to your browser. Earlier, you walked through the markup of an ASP.NET page. Let's see what the markup looks like in the browser.

View the HTML source of a page in Internet Explorer

1. From the **View** menu, select **Source**.

   The Notepad application opens with the markup shown in Listing 3-2. Let's walk through line by line.

   LISTING 3-2 ASP.NET Page Markup in the Browser

```
<!DOCTYPE html PUBLIC "-//W3C//DTD XHTML 1.0 Transitional//EN" http://www.w3.org/TR/
xhtml11/DTD/xhtml1-transitional.dtd>

<html xmlns="http://www.w3.org/1999/xhtml">

   <head><title>Untitled Page</title></head>

   <body>

      <form name="form1" method="post" action="Default1.aspx" id="form1">
      <div>

         <input type="hidden" name="__VIEWSTATE" id="__VIEWSTATE"
            value="/wEPDwUKMTUxMzcyMjQyN2RkabAobwSW3n9cpuJfgHHaqYkEQn0=" />

      </div>
      <div>

      </div>

      </form>

   </body>

</html>
```

The first thing you notice is that the <%@ Page Language="C#" %> and the <script runat="server"> markup is missing, and a <div> tag containing an <input> tag has appeared with new attributes, with one called *value* with a line of garble in it. What is going on? It's all ASP.NET.

Let's talk about what is happening. Refer to Figure 3-3. When you select the View In Browser command, Visual Web Developer starts up and configures the ASP.NET Development server for you as *http://localhost:portnumber*, pointed at the Project folder as the root. Like IIS in Windows Server 2003, the ASP.NET Development server is extended by ASP.NET, so when Visual Web Developer opens the browser to *http://localhost::portnumber4/Project /Default1.aspx*, the Web server receives the request to access Default.aspx from the browser, and ASP.NET takes over the request. It opens the Default.aspx page and processes the markup and code within the page. It processes only the code indicated to run on the server (hence, the *runat* attribute). Any code designated to run on the server is executed and re-moved from the final markup before it is returned to the browser. The standard markup that does not execute on the server will remain unchanged. The code executing on the server can also add or change the final markup before it is returned to the browser. In fact, that is what makes ASP.NET pages dynamic.

I know you might have questions about how this actually works. The best way to answer them is to show you.

Adding HTML to an ASP.NET Page

Let's walk through adding HTML markup to an ASP.NET page.

Close the browser window and return to the Visual Web Developer editor. Make sure the **Default1** tab is in front and active with the code displayed. Type, between the <div> tags enclosed in the <form> tag, **I Love Visual Web Developer!**. Your code should look like Listing 3-3.

LISTING 3-3 Default1 Code with Text

```
<%@ Page Language="C#" %>
<!DOCTYPE html PUBLIC "-//W3C//DTD XHTML 1.0 Transitional//EN" "http://www.w3.org/TR/xhtml1/
DTD/xhtml1-transitional.dtd">

<script runat="server">

</script>

<html xmlns="http://www.w3.org/1999/xhtml">

<head runat="server">
<title>Untitled Page</title>
  </head>
    <body>
     <form id="form1" runat="server">
```

```
    <div>
        I Love Visual Web Developer!
    </div>

    </form>

</body>
</html>
```

Select **View in Browser** from the **File** menu or from the standard toolbar. The browser will display the page shown in Figure 3-6. The text you added was passed through unchanged. You can select **Source** from the **View** menu in Internet Explorer to see the markup that was returned to the browser. Notice that the sentence you added is contained in the *second* pair of <div> tags. The *first* pair of <div> tags with the <input> tag and the *value* attribute with the garbled letters is above it. This was not added by you through code but by ASP.NET. *ViewState*; how it works is discussed in later chapters.

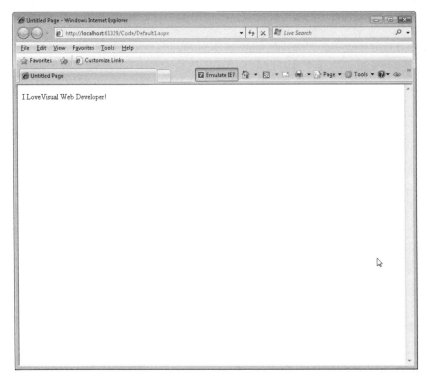

FIGURE 3-6 Default1 ASP.NET page with a sentence.

Close the browser window and return to the Visual Web Developer editor. You will add a line break to the sentence so that "I Love" appears on the first line and "Visual Web Developer!" appears on the other. Click the cursor right after the word *Love* in the editor. Type a space and then the < character. A list of HTML tags appears. This is the Visual Web Developer Microsoft IntelliSense feature. It will suggest valid HTML tags as you type. Continue to type

b-r->. As you type, you should see the selections change until the <br/> tag is completed for you, as shown in Figure 3-7. The <br/> tag is an HTML tag that inserts a single line break.

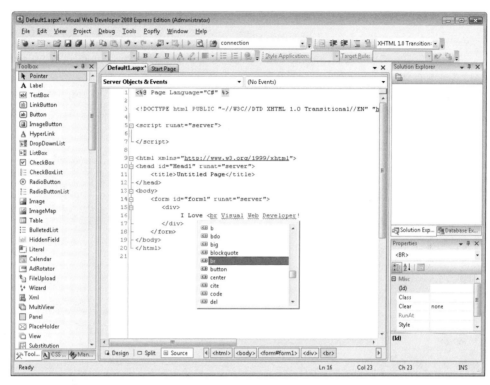

FIGURE 3-7 Visual Web Developer editor IntelliSense.

Your markup should look like Listing 3-4.

LISTING 3-4 Default1.aspx with a Line Break

```
<%@ Page Language="C#" %>
<!DOCTYPE html PUBLIC "-//W3C//DTD XHTML 1.0 Transitional//EN" "http://www.w3.org/TR/xhtml1/
DTD/xhtml1-transitional.dtd">

<script runat="server">

</script>

<html xmlns="http://www.w3.org/1999/xhtml">

<head runat="server">
<title>Untitled Page</title>
  </head>
    <body>
     <form id="form1" runat="server">

      <div>
         I Love Visual <br/> Web Developer!
```

```
    </div>

    </form>

  </body>
</html>
```

Select **View in Browser** from the **File** menu or from the standard toolbar. You should see the page as it appears in Figure 3-8. As you can see, the "I Love" appears on a line above "Visual Web Developer!" You can continue to add HTML tags to the text (bolding the sentence with a <b> tag or changing the font with the <font> tag) to see what happens. If you look at the source, you will see that your markup remains unchanged.

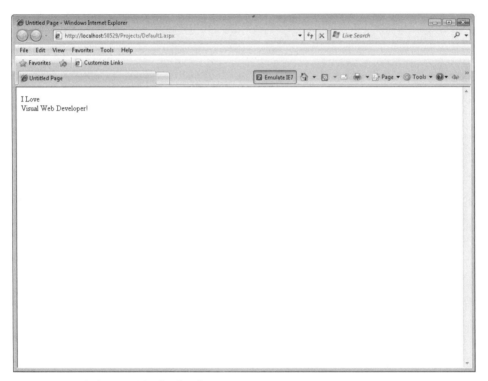

FIGURE 3-8 Default.aspx with a line break.

Adding JavaScript to an ASP.NET Page

Earlier in this chapter, I mentioned that the HTML on an ASP.NET page can be changed on the server before it is returned to the client. Before I show you how it can be changed on the server in ASP.NET with C#, I want to show you how it can be changed on the client in the browser with JavaScript. Every browser has JavaScript built in. It is a powerful option for you to use to create dynamic pages. It can also be added to your ASP.NET pages. Unlike C# code, which is executed on the server by the ASP.NET Web server extensions, JavaScript is executed on the client and is an extension of the browser.

You can add JavaScript to any ASP.NET page as you would any plain HTML page by using the <script> tag.

In the previous example, you typed the statement, "I Love Visual Web Developer!" into the page. In this example, you add the statement dynamically on the client in JavaScript.

Return to the Visual Web Developer editor and delete the statement you typed previously. Add the following markup and JavaScript code above the top <html> element:

```
<script type="text/javascript" language="javascript">

    document.write("I Love");
    document.write("<br/>");
    document.write("Visual Web Developer!");

</script>
```

The <script> tag is a standard HTML tag for wrapping JavaScript code. Everything typed within the tag is executable by the browser when the page is displayed on the page. The *document.write* is a standard JavaScript object and method to write HTML dynamically to the page displaying in the browser. Refer to Listing 3-5.

LISTING 3-5 JavaScript on an ASP.NET Page

```
<%@ Page Language="C#" %>
<!DOCTYPE html PUBLIC "-//W3C//DTD XHTML 1.0 Transitional//EN" "http://www.w3.org/TR/xhtml1/
DTD/xhtml1-transitional.dtd">


<script type="text/javascript" language="javascript">

    document.write("I Love");
    document.write("<br/>");
    document.write("Visual Web Developer!");

</script>

<script runat="server">

</script>

<html xmlns="http://www.w3.org/1999/xhtml">

<head runat="server">
<title>Untitled Page</title>
  </head>
    <body>
     <form id="form1" runat="server">
```

```
        <div>

        </div>

        </form>

    </body>
</html>
```

Select **View in Browser** from the **File** menu or from the standard toolbar. You should see the browser display the page, as Figure 3-8 illustrates. If you select **Source** from the **View** menu, you will notice something interesting—the source looks nearly identical to what is on the ASP.NET page. All the usual ASP.NET tags have been removed, and the <input> tag was still added. However, JavaScript code has not been stripped at all, and there is no sentence within the <div> tags.

This is because the code must be returned to the browser so it can execute the code within the <script> tags. The sentence is added dynamically, so it will not show on the page code—only in the browser.

JavaScript provides rich client capabilities that complement what you can do on the server with ASP.NET, so ASP.NET in no way interferes with what you can do in JavaScript. As you will see in later chapters, ASP.NET uses JavaScript to create rich Web interface experiences.

Adding HTML on the Server

As you have seen, with JavaScript, you can add HTML in the browser dynamically. I want to show you how it is done on the server.

I have talked about how server code is indicated by using the <script> tag with the *runat* attribute set to server. Another way is by enclosing .NET code with a starting <% and an ending %>. This means that code can be placed inline, even within other HTML tags. ASP.NET uses this technique not only to process code but also to indicate other preprocessing attributes.

Looking back at any of the listings, you will notice that the first line is exactly that: <%@ Page Language="C#" %>. This is a preprocessing directive that indicates what type of object ASP.NET is to create and what language to look for in its code. (So if you type Visual Basic code on a page indicated as C#, you will have errors.)

The best way to demonstrate this is by example. You previously used JavaScript to add a sentence to a page dynamically. Let's do it using C#.

Using the *Response* Object

Close the browser, if you have it open, and return to the Visual Web Developer editor. Delete the <script> tag containing the JavaScript code.

Add the following code between the two <div> tags contained by the <form> tag.

```
<%
  Response.Write("I Love");
  Response.Write("<br/>");
  Response.Write("Visual Web Developer!");
%>
```

The *Response* object, like the document object in JavaScript, is a special object built into ASP.NET that enables you to change the markup of a page dynamically after the request from the browser is received by the Web server and passed to ASP.NET. The *Response* object has a similar method called *Write*. The code looks very similar to the JavaScript code.

Look at Listing 3-6. Notice that the code must go in the exact place it will appear in the document. This is different from when you use JavaScript. Remember the code within the <% %> is inline.

LISTING 3-6 Adding HTML on the Server

```
<%@ Page Language="C#" %>
<!DOCTYPE html PUBLIC "-//W3C//DTD XHTML 1.0 Transitional//EN" "http://www.w3.org/TR/xhtml1/
DTD/xhtml1-transitional.dtd">


<script runat="server">

</script>

<html xmlns="http://www.w3.org/1999/xhtml">

<head runat="server">
<title>Untitled Page</title>
  </head>
    <body>
     <form id="form1" runat="server">

      <div>
          <%
            Response.Write("I Love");
            Response.Write("<br/>");
            Response.Write("Visual Web Developer!");
```

```
        %>
      </div>

    </form>

  </body>
</html>
```

Select **View in Browser** from the **File** menu or from the standard toolbar. You should see the browser display the page as Figure 3-8 illustrates. However, unlike the JavaScript example, if you select **Source** from the **View** menu, you will notice that the code is in the expected location and identical to Listing 3-6 where you typed the code in. Now imagine if you had some type of logic to determine what displayed on the screen. What if you connected to a database and created the interface based on the data you retrieved? Now you can understand the power of creating dynamic Web pages in ASP.NET.

Using the *Request* Object

In the previous example, you saw how the *Response* object is used in ASP.NET to write pages dynamically after the request from the browser is passed to ASP.NET. If the browser needs to pass information to the server, it uses query parameters. These are the value key pairs you typically see after URLs, for example: *http://www.moneycentral.msn.com/detail/ stock_quote?ipage=qdi&Symbol=MSFT.*

This example is a URL for the MSN Money central site to look up a stock quote for Microsoft. Everything after the ? in *http://www.moneycentral.msn.com/detail/stock_quote?* is a parameter name value pair separated by the & character: (*ipage=qdi,Symbol=MSFT*).

The *Request* object in ASP.NET helps you process these parameters, so let's define a parameter to show you how this works. Examine the following code:

```
  <%
Response.Write("I Love");
Response.Write("<br/>");
Response.Write(Request.QueryString["value"]);
%>
```

The first two lines are identical to the previous example. The third line is also similar, with the exception that the *Request* object is a parameter of the *Response.Write* method. The *Request* object is using its *QueryString* collection to retrieve a parameter called value.

> **Note** You can find out more about the *Request* and *Response* objects by searching the Visual Web Developer online help or by visiting the MSDN online documentation at *http://msdn2. microsoft.com/en-us/library/ms524948.aspx* and *http://msdn2.microsoft.com/en-us/library/ aa287829.aspx*, respectively.

This line will retrieve a parameter called value and write it in the HTML. If nothing is passed, nothing will be written to the HTML. The URL in this case should be *https:// locahost:SomePortNumber/Projects/Default1.aspx?value=SomeTextHere*, and the output should be:

```
I Love
SomeTextHere
```

Add the code to the Default1.aspx page so that your code looks exactly like Listing 3-7.

LISTING 3-7 Default1.aspx, Using the Request Object

```
<%@ Page Language="C#" %>
<!DOCTYPE html PUBLIC "-//W3C//DTD XHTML 1.0 Transitional//EN" "http://www.w3.org/TR/xhtml1/
DTD/xhtml1-transitional.dtd">

<script runat="server">

</script>

<html xmlns="http://www.w3.org/1999/xhtml">

<head runat="server">
<title>Untitled Page</title>
  </head>
    <body>
     <form id="form1" runat="server">

      <div>
          <%
            Response.Write("I Love");
            Response.Write("<br/>");
            Response.Write(Request.QueryString["value"]);
          %>
      </div>

     </form>

    </body>
</html>
```

Select **View in Browser** from the **File** menu or from the standard toolbar. You should see the browser display the page, as in Figure 3-9.

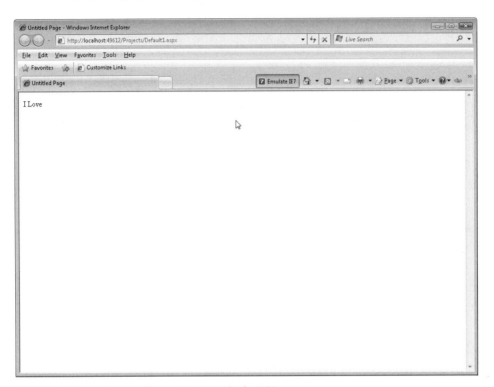

FIGURE 3-9 Default1.aspx with no parameters in the URL.

Notice that the URL has no parameters, so no text appears below the words, "I Love". Add the following text to the end of the URL of the page: **?value=Visual%20Web%20Developer**.

 Note The %20 characters between the words *Visual Web Developer* are required in URLs to represent spaces.

Press the **Enter** key to refresh the URL to show Default.aspx as it appears in Figure 3-10.

Change the parameter value to whatever you like to see what happens. You might also add more lines of code with conditional logic and more parameters to explore how powerful parameters can be.

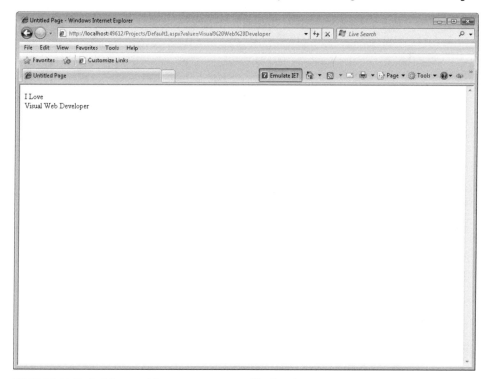

FIGURE 3-10 Default1.aspx with a parameter passed in the URL.

Creating Client Controls

You have added HTML content on the page dynamically on the client, using JavaScript, and on the server, using C#. Controls are the interface objects that enable you to interact with the user. As you might guess, there are server controls and client controls. Client controls are used by JavaScript. Let's examine client controls.

Visual Web Developer provides a rich editing environment to create controls. Client controls are called HTML controls in Visual Web Developer.

To create a HTML control

1. Click the **Toolbox**, and then click the **Auto Hide** pin to keep it visible. Scroll down to the HTML section and expand it.

2. Click **Split** at the bottom of the **Default1.aspx** editor to split the screen in two horizontally. You will see the faint outline of the <div> tag in the interface designer. Click inside the outline to see the <div> tag become highlighted in the code editor.

3. Click the **Input (Button)** option in the **Toolbox**. Drag and drop the control inside the <div> outline on the designer.

You should see the <input> tag highlight in the code editor, as in Figure 3-11.

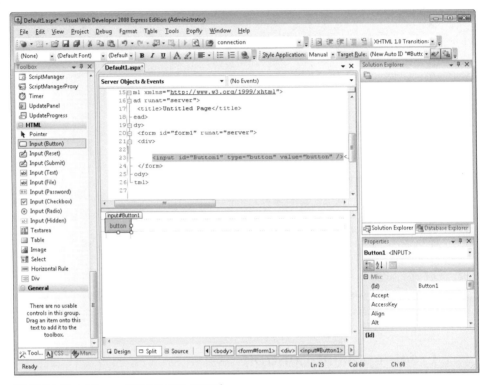

FIGURE 3-11 Adding an HTML Button control.

The code in the editor should look exactly like Listing 3-8.

LISTING 3-8 Markup with HTML Button Added

```
<%@ Page Language="C#" %>
<!DOCTYPE html PUBLIC "-//W3C//DTD XHTML 1.0 Transitional//EN" "http://www.w3.org/TR/
xhtml1/DTD/xhtml1-transitional.dtd">



<script runat="server">

</script>

<html xmlns="http://www.w3.org/1999/xhtml">

<head runat="server">
<title>Untitled Page</title>
```

```
</head>
  <body>
   <form id="form1" runat="server">

    <div>
       <input id="Button1" type="button" value="button" />
    </div>

   </form>

  </body>
</html>
```

4. Save the page, and then select View in Browser from the File menu or from the standard toolbar.

   You should see the browser display the page as shown in Figure 3-12.

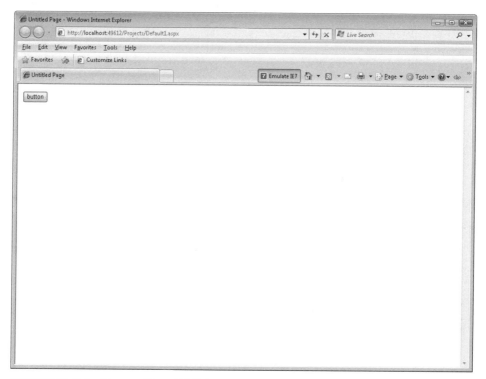

FIGURE 3-12 Default1.aspx with an HTML button.

You can click the button, but nothing will happen, so add some code to do something simple. I have been trying to avoid using the standard programming book cliché, but I can't resist—you will create some code to display a JavaScript alert and say, "Hello World!"

As you did in the earlier JavaScript example, you must add the <script> tag back with attributes to indicate that JavaScript client code needs to be executed.

```
<script type="text/javascript" language="javascript">
  function SayHello()
  {
    alert("Hello World!");
  }
</script>
```

Add the preceding code to the page as you did before. The JavaScript code defines a function called *SayHello* that will be called when you click the button. Then a JavaScript alert function will display a dialog box that states, "Hello World!"

You have to hook the HTML Button control click event to the JavaScript code. You do this by adding the *onclick* attribute to the <input> tag and setting it to call the *SayHello* function.

```
<input id="Button1" type="button" value="button" onclick="SayHello();"/>
```

Edit the <input> tag until it looks like the preceding code. When you are finished, the code should look like Listing 3-9.

LISTING 3-9 Default1.aspx to Show "Hello World!" dialog box

```
<%@ Page Language="C#" %>
<!DOCTYPE html PUBLIC "-//W3C//DTD XHTML 1.0 Transitional//EN" "http://www.w3.org/TR/xhtml1/
DTD/xhtml1-transitional.dtd">

<script type="text/javascript" language="javascript">

function SayHello()
{
    alert("Hello World!");
}

</script>

<script runat="server">

</script>

<html xmlns="http://www.w3.org/1999/xhtml">

<head runat="server">
<title>Untitled Page</title>
  </head>
    <body>
      <form id="form1" runat="server">

        <div>
          <input id="Button1" type="button" value="button" onclick="SayHello();"/>
        </div>
```

```
        </form>

    </body>
</html>
```

Save the page, and then select **View in Browser** from the **File** menu or from the standard toolbar. You should see the browser display the page shown in Figure 3-13. Click the button and you will see a dialog appear with "Hello World!"

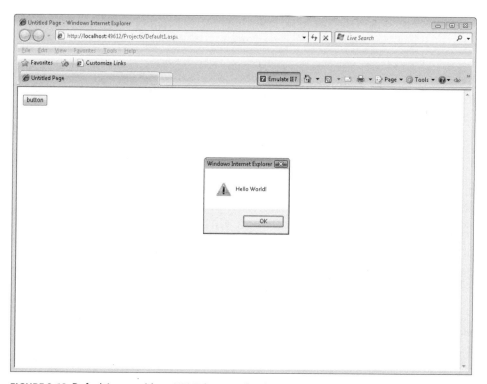

FIGURE 3-13 Default1.aspx with an HTML button after being clicked.

Creating Server Controls

Now that you have created a client control and added JavaScript code to display an alert, let's do the same thing but with a server control and C#. The limitation you need to understand is that server controls display on the client exactly like an HTML control, but the code attached to it executes on the server. When the button is clicked on the client, the event is sent back to the server for execution, so displaying dialog boxes is not possible.

However, there are other ways to achieve the same goal.

To create a Button server control

1. Click the **Toolbox**, and then click the **Auto Hide** pin to keep it visible. Scroll up to the **Standard** section and expand it.

2. Click the **Split** button at the bottom of the **Default1.aspx** editor to split the screen in two horizontally. You will see the faint outline of the <div> tag in the interface designer. Click inside the outline to see the <div> tag become highlighted in the code editor.

3. Click **Button** in the **Toolbox**. Drag and drop the control inside the <div> outline on the designer. You should see the <asp:Button> tag highlight in the code editor. See Figure 3-14.

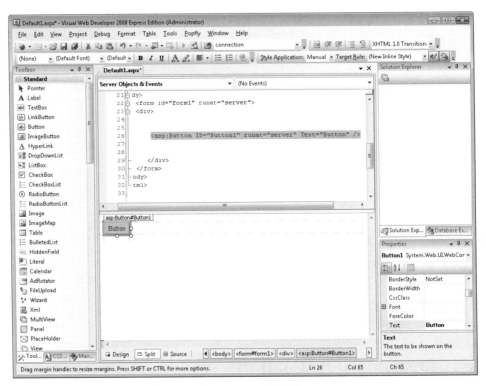

FIGURE 3-14 Default1.aspx with a server Button control added.

The tag is different for server button controls: <asp:Button>. It has an *ID*, a *Text*, and a *runat* attribute set to *server*. You know you can't display a dialog box, so you will use a Label server control to display the message.

To create a Label server control

1. Click the **Toolbox**, and then click the **Auto Hide** pin to keep it visible. Scroll up to the **Standard** section and expand it.

2. Click **Label** in the **Toolbox**. Drag and drop the control to the right side of **Button**.

   You should see the <asp:Label> tag highlight in the code editor. See Figure 3-15.

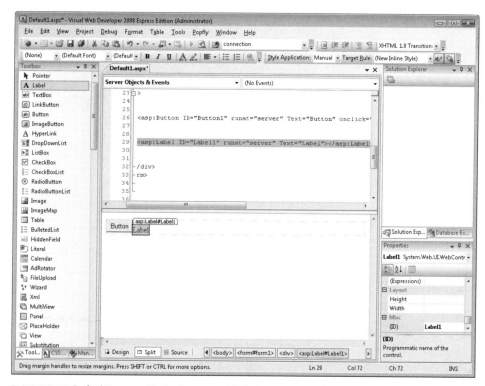

FIGURE 3-15 Default1.aspx with the Button and Label server controls.

Now that you have added a Label, you must create the code to set the Label Text field when the button is clicked. You can double-click **Button** in the Visual Web Developer designer to add the following code to the page.

```
<script runat="server">
    protected void Button1_Click1(object sender, EventArgs e)
    {

    }
</script>
```

The <script> tag is used with a *runat* attribute set to *server*. The code inside is an empty event handler for the button called Button1_Click1. Add the following code:

```
Label1.Text = "Hello World!";
```

This code will set the label's Text field.

Your page should look like Listing 3-10.

LISTING 3-10 Default1.aspx with the Button and Label Server Controls

```
<%@ Page Language="C#" %>
<!DOCTYPE html PUBLIC "-//W3C//DTD XHTML 1.0 Transitional//EN" "http://www.w3.org/TR/xhtml1/
DTD/xhtml1-transitional.dtd">


<script runat="server">
    protected void Button1_Click1(object sender, EventArgs e)
    {
        Label1.Text = "Hello World!";
    }
</script>

<html xmlns="http://www.w3.org/1999/xhtml">

<head runat="server">
<title>Untitled Page</title>
  </head>
    <body>
     <form id="form1" runat="server">

      <div>
        <asp:Button ID="Button1" runat="server" Text="Button" onclick="Button1_Click1"/>
        <asp:Label ID="Label1" runat="server" Text="Label"></asp:Label>
      </div>

     </form>

   </body>
</html>
```

Save the page, and then select **View in Browser** from the **File** menu or from the standard toolbar. You should see the browser display the page as shown in Figure 3-16. Label is set to its default value of *Label*.

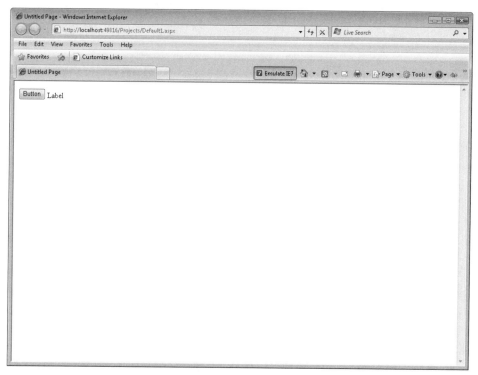

FIGURE 3-16 Default1.aspx with server Button and Label set to the default value.

Click the button to see the Label's value change to "Hello World!" See Figure 3-17.

FIGURE 3-17   Default1.aspx with server Button clicked and Label set to "Hello World!"

Summary

In this chapter, you learned the basics of ASP.NET pages. You learned that Web forms are the heart of ASP.NET pages. You learned that you can create HTML controls in the browser that can be programmed by JavaScript. You learned how to add HTML dynamically by using JavaScript on the client and C# on the server, and you learned how to create server controls and program them with C#. Now that you understand the basics of ASP.NET pages, you can begin creating Web sites in Chapter 4.

Chapter 4
Creating Your First Web Site

After completing this chapter, you will be able to

- Define requirements by using stories.

- Create a Web site.

- Understand code behind.

- Run and build a Web site.

- Use the ASP.NET Site Administration Tool to configure site security.

- Show where user security information is stored in *ASPNETDB.MDF*.

- Use the *Login* server controls for Login, Login Status, and Changing Password.

In this chapter, you begin the development of your personal portal. You'll build this example throughout the rest of this book.

Defining Requirements

The first thing you need to do when you are building a Web site is gather the requirements. Requirements are statements, formal or informal, that include a system's functionality and features.

For example: The system shall contain a way for users to log in. The system shall contain a way for the user to change his or her password.

In this formal way, the system is the focus. Requirements are usually numbered and cross-referenced throughout interconnected requirements documents. Large systems can have requirements documents that number in the hundreds and thousands of pages. This is the way I learned back when I first started programming in the early 1990s. Many organizations do this today, and it's still the most comprehensive way to capture requirements. Formal requirements documentation is also best used in organizations that have solid processes and procedures to facilitate their development and review.

Over the years, new ways of gathering requirements have evolved. Although the formal requirement documentation process was system- and functionality-centric, new, less-formal requirements documentation processes focus on users. This technique puts users at the center of what is required by examining their goals. This technique is called *persona stories*. You can read more about personas, and how they are used to define requirements, in the book *About Face 2.0* (Wiley Press, 2003) by Alan Cooper and Robert Riemann.

The Personal Portal Story

Eric is a consultant. He travels 70 percent of the time. When he is traveling, he has access to wireless Internet connections in airports, customer sites, and hotels. He has a notebook for work and tries to keep his personal life and work separate.

However, his personal life is just as important as his work life, so he needs tools to keep his personal life organized. He uses a variety of Internet tools to help him. He uses Microsoft Virtual Earth maps to find hotels, customer sites, and places to eat and visit. He reads news by using RSS feeds through a browser. He stores files on a virtual drive service and uses a site to manage his personal to-do list from his wife as well as his other tasks. He uses Internet social bookmarking services such as del.icio.us to store links, too. He uses Flickr to store photos of places he visits to share with his family.

His major problem with all these tools that make his life easier is that they are not in one place. He wants a portal that focuses on his life and things he needs to track and manage. He needs a personal portal.

In his personal portal, Eric wants security, but he wants the ability to grant access to family and friends. He also wants to change his password easily. In his personal portal, he wants all the features and functionality of the different services and sites he uses every day—to-dos, news feeds, maps, remote storage, links, and photos.

Creating a Web Site

Now that you know what you want to build, it's time to start building it. You can create a Web site by using one of the four available templates. Start Visual Web Developer. From the **File** menu, choose **New Web Site**.

The New Web Site dialog box appears, as shown in Figure 4-1. You can search online for new templates, or you can select one of the four installed templates: ASP.NET Web Site, ASP.NET Web services, Empty Web Site, and WCF (Windows Communication Foundation) Service.

You don't want to create a service or an empty Web site, so select **ASP.NET Web Site**.

You want to create a File System project because it doesn't require Internet Information Services (IIS) or a remote host. Type the name of your site, **PersonalPortal**, at the end of the directory listed in the text box. (The directory should be the location of your Documents folder).

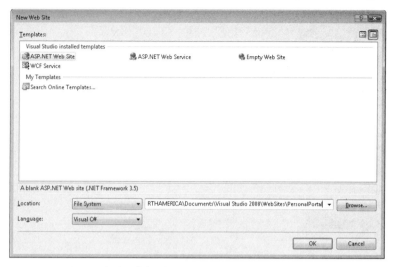

FIGURE 4-1 New Web Site dialog box.

Visual Web Developer Project Types

- **File System**   In a file system Web site, you are not required to run IIS or Microsoft Windows Server 2003 on your computer. Instead, you can test pages by using the ASP.NET Development Server as explored in Chapter 3, "Creating Your First ASP.NET Page."

- **FTP**   This type enables you to open and edit Web sites that are available on a File Transfer Protocol (FTP) server. This is a typical scenario if your Web site is located on a hosting site.

- **HTTP**   This type enables you to open a remote Web site that uses IIS but is on another computer that you can access over a local area network. The remote computer must have IIS installed and be configured with Microsoft FrontPage 2002 server extensions.

Visual Web Developer should open to the Default.aspx page markup on a new tab. Before you look further at the project, click the **Start Page** tab and see that PersonalPortal is now listed under **Recent Projects**. When you open Visual Web Developer in the future, you can click it to open your project. You can also open recent files and projects from the File menu and the Recent Files and Recent Projects menu items, respectively. The Recent Projects screen is illustrated in Figure 4-2.

FIGURE 4-2 PersonalPortal listed on Recent Projects.

Return to the Default.aspx page (see Figure 4-3) and examine the project. In Solution Explorer, you have a list of items. The first item is a truncated path to the PersonalPortal project. Notice that if you click an item in Solution Explorer, the Properties window will fill with property values about the item.

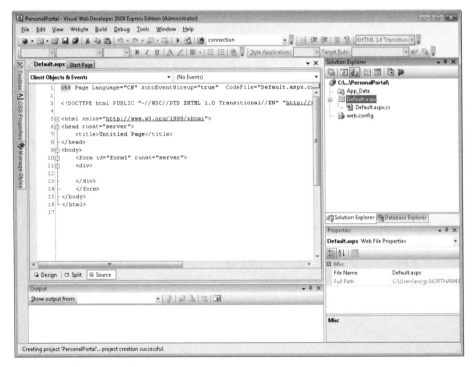

FIGURE 4-3 The PersonalPortal project.

Clicking the first item in the list, open the project item and look at the **Properties** window. (See Figure 4-4.) The properties are categorized, and you can edit available items (not dimmed). In this case, PersonalPortal has been assigned the unique port number, 49766, which is not editable. However, three other properties, Always Start When Debugging, Use Dynamic Ports, and Virtual Path are editable. Clicking the property name displays tips about the property. Until you know more about a property (you can look it up using online help), changing them isn't recommended.

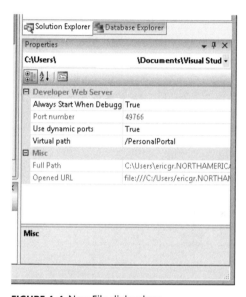

FIGURE 4-4 New File dialog box.

Referring back to Figure 4-3, you might be wondering where these items are located. Are they bundled in a project file, or are they on your hard drive somewhere? Chapter 1, "Introducing Visual Web Developer 2008," explored the different directories that are created when Visual Web Developer is installed. You used these directories when you created the PersonalPortal project.

Open your **Documents** folder in Windows Vista or your **MyDocuments** folder in Windows XP. Find the Visual Studio 2008 folder and open the Projects folder inside it. You should see the PersonalPortal project file as shown in Figure 4-5.

Return to the Visual Studio 2008 folder and open the WebSites folder and the PersonalPortal folder that have been created. You will see the App_Data folder with the Default.aspx, Default.aspx.cs, and Web.config files. (See Figure 4-6.)

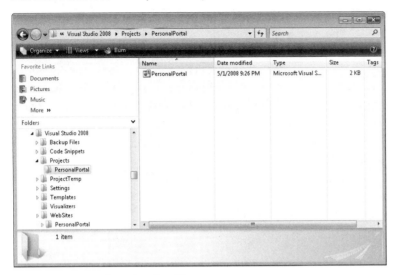

FIGURE 4-5 PersonalPortal project file.

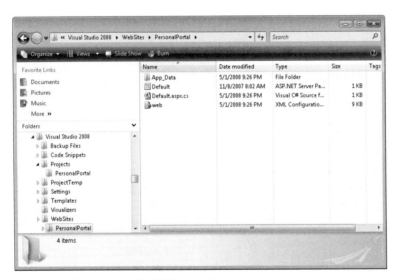

FIGURE 4-6 PersonalPortal in WebSites folder.

This is where your Web sites will be run from. This is the location the ASP.NET Development server will use to create a virtual path to run your Web site. If you need to add files to be used by your Web site, you drop them here.

If you want to back up your project, you can use your project's Projects and WebSites folders to package it.

Understanding Code Behind

You might have noticed the Default.aspx.cs file in the PersonalPortal WebSites directory. You can also find the file underneath the Default.aspx page in Solution Explorer. This is the code behind file. In Chapter 3, when you created your first ASP.NET page, you learned how to designate code to be run on the server. This code was written inline with HTML, using the <script> tag or enclosed in <% and %>.

Adding code to your pages like this is fine when the code is simple and short. However, as code becomes longer and more complex, it can become difficult to maintain. Code behind is a way to separate code from markup to ease developing and maintaining complex code.

If you look at the code of Default.aspx in Listing 4-1, it looks very similar to the page you created in Chapter 3.

LISTING 4-1 DEFAULT.ASPX

```
<%@ Page Language="C#" AutoEventWireup="true"  CodeFile="Default.aspx.cs" Inherits="_
Default" %>

<!DOCTYPE html PUBLIC "-//W3C//DTD XHTML 1.0 Transitional//EN" "http://www.w3.org/TR/xhtml1/
DTD/xhtml1-transitional.dtd">

<html xmlns="http://www.w3.org/1999/xhtml">
<head runat="server">

    <title>Untitled Page</title>

</head>

<body>

    <form id="form1" runat="server">

    <div>


    </div>

    </form>

</body>

</html>
```

All the lines are the same except the first line. The three attributes are *AutoEventWireup*, *Codefile*, and *Inherits*.

AutoEventWireup is set to *true*. Visual Web Developer, by default, generates code to bind events to their event-handler methods (more about generated code later).

The *CodeFile* attribute value is set to *Default.aspx.cs*. This attribute tells Visual Web Developer to compile the code in this file. Listing 4-2 shows the code in Default.aspx.cs. A function called *Page_Load* loads the page when it's first started.

> **Note** If you want to learn more about the dozens of events that ASP.NET pages have, you can read about them at *http://msdn.microsoft.com/library/4w3ex9c2.aspx*.

LISTING 4-2 DEFAULT.ASPX.CS

```
using System;
using System.Configuration;
using System.Data;
using System.Linq;
using System.Web;
using System.Web.Security;
using System.Web.UI;
using System.Web.UI.HtmlControls;
using System.Web.UI.WebControls;
using System.Web.UI.WebControls.WebParts;
using System.Xml.Linq;

public partial class _Default : System.Web.UI.Page
{
    protected void Page_Load(object sender, EventArgs e)
    {

    }
}
```

Understanding Namespaces

Namespaces are an important part of writing C#. Namespaces organize .NET objects so that you can find them easily. An important namespace for you to learn more about is the *System. Web* namespace. You can read more about it at *http://msdn.microsoft.com/library/system. web.aspx*.

Running a Web Site

Now you have walked through the site and seen what the items are in a project and where they reside on your hard drive. Run your personal portal by clicking **Start Debugging** on the standard toolbar. (See Figure 4-7.)

The first thing you will be presented with is the Debugging Not Enabled dialog box. (See Figure 4-8.) The dialog box gives you a choice; the default is to change the Web.config file. The Web.config file is in your project file. You'll return to that later. For now, leave the default value and click **OK**.

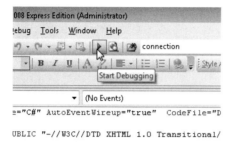

FIGURE 4-7 Start Debugging.

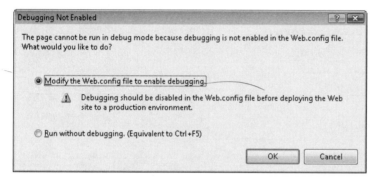

FIGURE 4-8 Debugging Not Enabled dialog box.

The personal portal appears in the Web browser as shown in Figure 4-9. The tab in Internet Explorer is set to the name of the page.

FIGURE 4-9 New File dialog box.

Without closing the browser window, bring the Visual Web Developer windows to the front. Notice some menus are disabled, as shown in Figure 4-10. You can also change code or markup in the editor, but when you are in debug mode in Visual Web Developer, any changes to code files or markup won't be visible until the project is stopped and restarted.

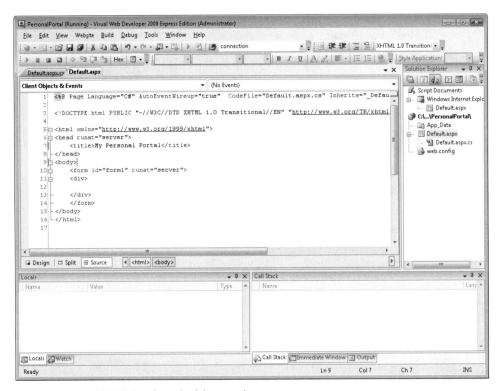

FIGURE 4-10 Visual Web Developer in debug mode.

Several other windows with tabs display at the bottom of Visual Web Developer. They are the Locals, Watch, Call Stack, Immediate Window, and Output windows. The windows aid in debugging code while it is running. You will explore these windows as you develop the personal portal.

FIGURE 4-11 Run, Pause, Stop, and Restart buttons.

Figure 4-11 shows the Run, Pause, Stop, and Restart buttons on the standard toolbar. Pausing the project will render the Web site unresponsive until you restart or stop the project.

Stop the personal portal by clicking **Stop** or closing the browser window. Remember the dialog box that appeared before you ran the project (Figure 4-8), asking whether you wanted to modify the Web.config file? Let's go find where the change was made.

The Web.config file is the central XML file that enables you to configure settings for your Web site. Every ASP.NET Web site has one. In this case, it was setting the project in a debug mode. Double-click the Web.config file in **Solution Explorer**. Scroll down the screen until you find the tag called <compilation debug="true">. Visual Web Developer sets this attribute for you, or you can do so by changing the value of the debug attribute.

> **Note** You can read more about ASP.NET configuration files at *http://msdn.microsoft.com/library/ aa719558.aspx.*

Building a Web Site

When you run your project, there is no guarantee that it will start, especially if you have errors (bugs) in your code. The Visual Web Developer editor does a lot to help eliminate errors with Microsoft IntelliSense and error checking as you type. As you develop your personal portal, you will see more of this. However, this is not the only way to make sure your project will run successfully. You can build your project without running it. (In fact, before you run your project, it is built; if no errors are found, your project is launched.)

You can build your project before you run it to check all your work by using the Build menu. You can build a single page, build the entire Web site, or rebuild the entire Web site.

With the Default.aspx page selected, click the **Build** menu and select **Build Web Site**. (See Figure 4-12.)

FIGURE 4-12 The Build menu.

Below the Visual Web Developer code window is the Output window, which displays messages from Visual Web Developer. When Visual Web Developer attempts to compile a site or page, the results appear here. Figure 4-13 shows a successful build of a personal portal. Because you haven't added any code, this is an expected result.

FIGURE 4-13 The Output window indicating a successful build.

Return to Visual Web Developer and open the Default.aspx.cs page in the editor. Type the *Response* object into the *Page_Load* function. (You will also have help from IntelliSense because it pops open as you type.) Note that there is no method call or ending, as required by C# statements. This is an error.

LISTING 4-3 Default.aspx.cs

```
USING SYSTEM;
USING SYSTEM.CONFIGURATION;
USING SYSTEM.DATA;
USING SYSTEM.LINQ;
USING SYSTEM.WEB;
USING SYSTEM.WEB.SECURITY;
USING SYSTEM.WEB.UI;
USING SYSTEM.WEB.UI.HTMLCONTROLS;
USING SYSTEM.WEB.UI.WEBCONTROLS;
USING SYSTEM.WEB.UI.WEBCONTROLS.WEBPARTS;
USING SYSTEM.XML.LINQ;

PUBLIC PARTIAL CLASS _DEFAULT : SYSTEM.WEB.UI.PAGE
{
    PROTECTED VOID PAGE_LOAD(OBJECT SENDER, EVENTARGS E)
    {
        RESPONSE


    }
}
```

As soon as you type the *Reponse* object and press **Enter** or the spacebar, a jagged line appears after the *Response* object. This is the Visual Web Developer inline error checking, indicating that you have an error in your code. (See Figure 4-14.)

```
14  {
15      protected void Page_Load(object sender, EventArgs e)
16      {
17          Response
18
19      }
20  }
21
```

FIGURE 4-14 Visual Web Developer inline error checking.

Let's build the Web site anyway, just to see what happens. From the **Build** menu, select **Build Web Site**. This time, an Error List window shows one error with no warnings or messages, as Figure 4-15 illustrates. In it, you have a list with the error's description and the file it's located in, including the line and column and which project it belongs to. Double-clicking the line will take you to the error's exact location.

Click the **Output** tab; you will see the failed results of the build.

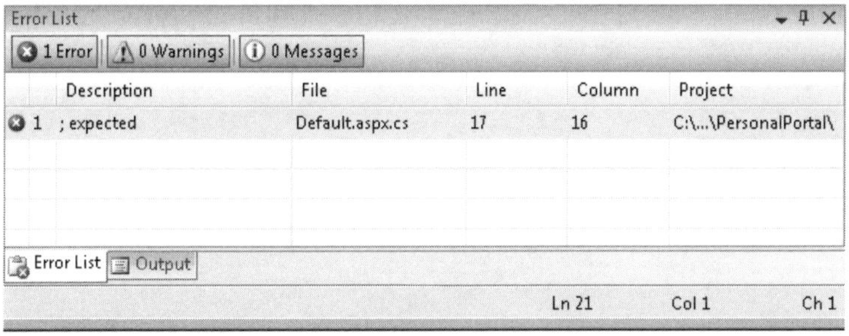

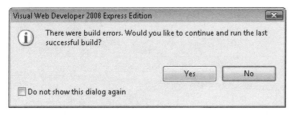

FIGURE 4-15 Visual Web Developer inline error checking.

Let's see what happens when you run the project anyway. Click **Run** on the standard toolbar. Figure 4-16 shows the dialog box that appears when you try to run a project with errors.

FIGURE 4-16 Build errors dialog box.

You have a choice of whether you want to run the project based on the last successful build. If you click Yes, the personal portal will not reflect any changes you made since you last ran the project.

Using the ASP.NET Site Administration Tool

Now that you know how to run and build your personal portal, you can learn about configuring it. The ASP.NET Site Administration tool is a Web application, installed with Visual Web Developer, that enables you to configure a very important requirement of the personal portal: security.

Based on your personal portal requirements, a login page is required to secure the site. Before you can do that, you must enable security for the site and create users, the first of which is you.

Note New Web sites created with Visual Web Developer don't have security enabled. Anonymous access is the default (that is, anyone can access the site without a userid or password).

You can start the ASP.NET Site Administration tool from Solution Explorer or from the Web site menu and ASP.NET Configuration.

To open the ASP.NET Administration tool, click the icon in **Solution Explorer**. (See Figure 4-17.)

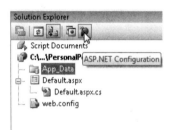

FIGURE 4-17 Starting the ASP.NET Configuration tool from Solution Explorer.

A browser window will open, and a Web site will appear that is running in the Visual Developer built-in Web server (Figure 4-18). There are four tabs, labeled Home, Security, Application, and Provider.

FIGURE 4-18 ASP.NET Web Site Administration tool running in a browser.

On the Home tab, you can see the reference to the personal portal as Application and your user name as the Current User Name. (I blocked out my user name for security reasons.)

- **Security Tab**   On the Security tab, you set up and edit users, roles, and access permissions for your site. This is where you will set things up, but let's briefly talk about the other two tabs.

- **Application Tab**   The Application tab enables you to manage your application's configuration settings such as the site's default e-mail server, Application Status, and Debugging and Tracing settings. You won't be doing any configuration here.

- **Provider Tab**   The Provider tab enables you to specify where and how to store administration data used by your Web site. You won't be looking at this functionality until Chapter 13, "Deploying Your Web Site," when you deploy your Web site.

Configuring Site Security

The Security tab is where you start your setup.

To set up Security on the personal portal

1. Click the **Security** tab.

2. In the **Users** section, click the **Select authentication type** link. (See Figure 4-19).

FIGURE 4-19 Clicking the Select Authentication Type link.

3. Select **From the internet** (Figure 4-20). Click **Done**.

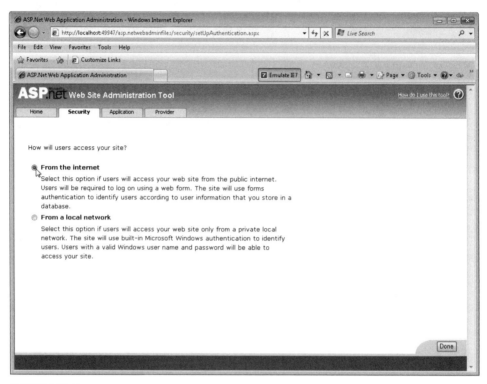

FIGURE 4-20 User access page.

After you select the user access level, you are returned to the Security tab's first page. Notice the two new links you can use to create and manage users. (See Figure 4-21.)

FIGURE 4-21 Create User and Manage Users links.

The first person you must add is you.

To add a user

1. In the Security tab's **Users** section, click **Create User.**

2. When the Create User dialog box appears (Figure 4-22), fill in the following displayed fields:

- User Name
- Password (The password must be seven characters long and contain one non-alphanumeric value.)
- Security Question
- Security Answer

3. Select the **Active** user check box to activate the user on the Web site.

4. Click **Create User**.

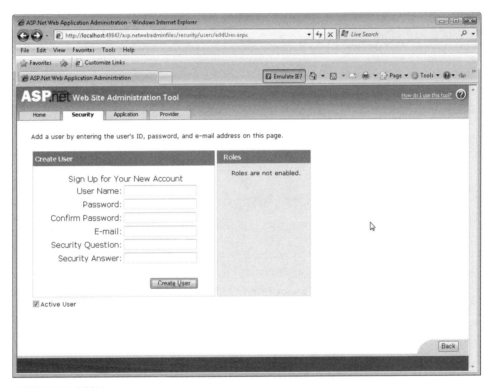

FIGURE 4-22 Add User page.

You can create as many users as you need in this way. After you have entered all the users, you can see the list of users you created by clicking Manage Users from the Users section of the Security tab.

The screen that displays, shown in Figure 4-23, after you click Manage Users organizes the list of users by name. It also enables you to search for users.

To edit an existing user, click the **Edit user** link to the right of the user name. To delete a user, click the **Delete user** link.

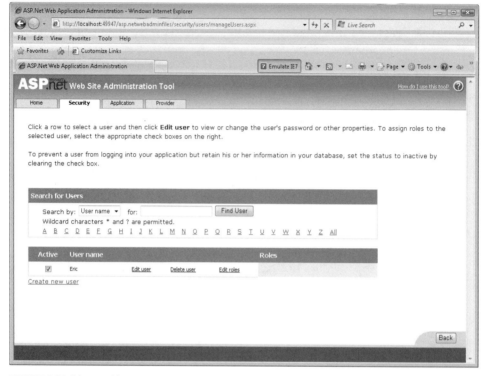

FIGURE 4-23 Manage Users screen.

Now that the users of your site have been created, you might be wondering what is going on behind the scenes. Where is the user information stored? How is it used?

Examining the ASP.NET Configuration Database

The ASP.NET Web Site Administration tool uses a database to store information about security and users. This database can be deployed to a public Web site host after you finish development. You will learn more about that in Chapter 13. You can find this database in the App_Data folder in Solution Explorer. See Figure 4-24. If you don't see the database in the folder, you might have to refresh the folder by right-clicking **App_Data** and selecting **Refresh Folder**.

ASPNETDB.MDF is a database. Visual Web Developer has built-in functionality that enables you to create, edit, and browse databases. This functionality is available from Database Explorer.

FIGURE 4-24 Selecting *ASPNETDB.MDF*.

To browse for a user in the *ASPNETDB.MDF* database, using Database Explorer

1. Right-click **ASPNETDB.MDF** and select **Open**. Database Explorer opens. (See Figure 4-25.)

FIGURE 4-25 ASP*NETDB.MDF* in Database Explorer.

2. Double-click the **Tables** folder to open the tables contained in the database.

   You'll see more about tables in Chapter 8, "Working with Databases."

3. Find the **aspnet_User** table.

4. Right-click the **aspnet_Users** table and select **Show Table Data**. (See Figure 4-26.)

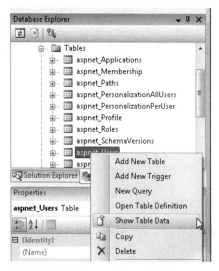

FIGURE 4-26 Selecting Show Table Data.

A grid with all the users you added will display. Several fields display, such as *UserName*. (See Figure 4-27.) Do not edit the data. This is where ASP.NET goes to verify security data. There are many other tables in *ASPNETDB.MDF*. Select a few more and see what you can find.

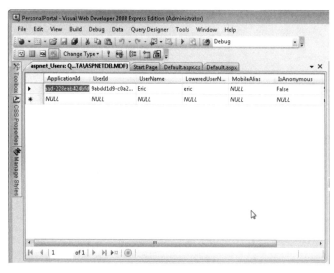

FIGURE 4-27 List of users in aspnet_Users.

You have created your first user and, now, you must enforce your security settings. You need a login page.

Creating a Login Page

The default page is where you want to have all your functionality. Typically, private Web sites allocate the functionality of logging in to a separate page called a Login page.

ASP.NET has several server controls that, without writing any code, can handle all the functionality of validating users of your site.

Start Visual Web Developer and open the PersonalPortal project. Right-click the **PersonalPortal** project in **Solution Explorer** and select **Add New Item**. (See Figure 4-28.)

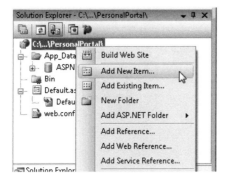

FIGURE 4-28 Selecting Add New Item in the PersonalPortal project.

The Add New Item dialog box appears, shown in Figure 4-29. You have dozens of objects to choose from. Select **Web Form** from the list and type **Login.aspx** in the **Name** field. Leave Place Code In Separate File selected.

FIGURE 4-29 Add Item dialog box, creating the Login.aspx page.

Select **Login.aspx** and make sure it is set on the design surface. Open the **toolbox** and pin it. Scroll down and open the **Login** section of the t**oolbox**. Drag and drop the **Login** server control to the **Login** design surface within the outlined *<div>* element. (See Figure 4-30.)

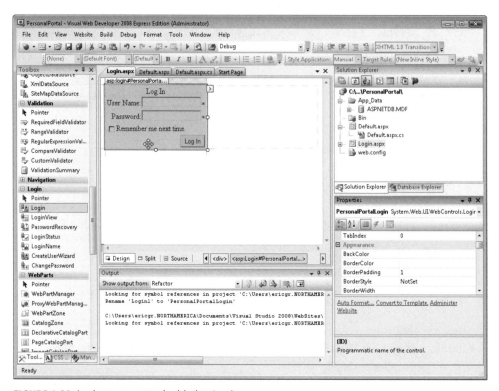

FIGURE 4-30 *Login* server control added to Login.aspx.

Click the server control and examine the values in the **Properties** window. Many of the items on the *Login* server control can be changed, such as the labels for UserName, Password, and LogIn. You can experiment with the settings later.

The Default.aspx page is configured to be the page the Web server opens when the site runs. Because you want users to log in before they have access to the site, you must make the Login.aspx page the first page to start.

You can set this behavior by right-clicking the **Login.aspx** window in **Solution Explorer** and selecting **Set as start page**, as shown in Figure 4-31. You can do this for any page on your site.

FIGURE 4-31 Setting the Start page for the personal portal.

Before you run the site and test the security, you must change one setting on the *Login* server control. Select the **Login** server control in the **Login.aspx** design surface. In the Properties window, find **DestinationPageURL** in the **Behavior** section of the **Login** server control properties. Click the ellipsis button to display the **Select URL** dialog box. (See Figure 4-32.) Select **Default.aspx** and click **OK**.

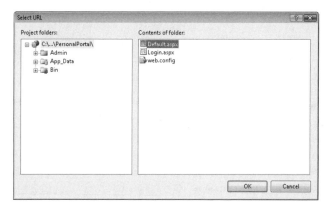

FIGURE 4-32 Select URL dialog box.

If the login is successful, the Default.aspx page will display. Now that you have everything set up, let's run it.

Click **Run** on the standard toolbar to run the project. If your project has no errors, the browser will open with the *Login* server control displayed.

First, try to enter an invalid user ID and password. Type your user name in the *UserName* field. In this case, I typed "Eric". Next, type an invalid password in the *Password* field. Click **Log In**.

> **Note** You know by examining the *ASPNETDB.MDF* database earlier in this chapter that ASP.NET will look up the user name and password data from the aspnet_Users table.

An error displays in red below the Remember Me Next Time check box. (See Figure 4-33.)

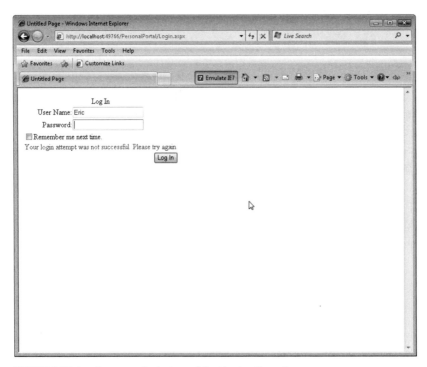

FIGURE 4-33 Log In server displaying a failed login attempt.

Now that you know how the *Login* server control will fail, enter the correct user name and password in the respective fields. (See Figure 4-34.) Note that the password field does not show the characters of the password.

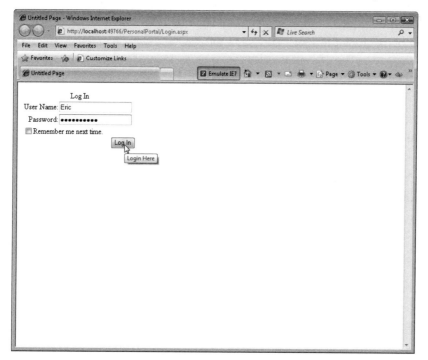

FIGURE 4-34 Entering the correct user name and password in the *Login* server control.

After you enter the correct user name and password, you are redirected to the Default.aspx page. At this time, nothing is displayed on the Default.aspx page.

Using the *LoginName* and *LoginStatus* Server Controls

On many Web sites, when users are logged in, their user name appears on the site along with the ability to log out of the site. Fortunately, ASP.NET has *LoginName* and *LoginStatus* server controls that do just that. The *LoginName* server control displays the name of the logged-on user. The *LoginStatus* server control is a dynamic link that enables the user to log out of the site. On a Web site, these controls are beside each other.

To add the *LoginName* and *LoginStatus* server controls to the Default.aspx page

1. Close the browser window and stop running the site. In Visual Web Developer, double-click **Default.aspx** to open it in the editor.

2. Select the **Design** tab in the editor to show the design surface.

3. Open the **toolbox** and scroll down to the **Login** section.

4. Drag the **LoginName** server control to the outlined *<div>* element in the Default.aspx design surface. The placeholder for the control should display [UserName]. Place the cursor before [UserName] and type **Welcome**. Place the cursor after [UserName] and type an exclamation mark: **!**.

5. Return to the **Login** section in the **toolbox** and drag the **LoginStatus** server control to **Default.aspx** to the right of the exclamation mark. The placeholder for the control will be a link called *Login*.

6. Click the **LoginStatus** control on the design surface. Move to the **Behavior** section of the **LoginStatus** properties in the **Properties** window.

7. From the drop-down list for the **LogoutAction** property, select **RedirectToLoginPage**.

8. Using the ellipsis and URL picker dialog box, set the **LogutPageURL** to **Login.aspx**. (See Figure 4-35.)

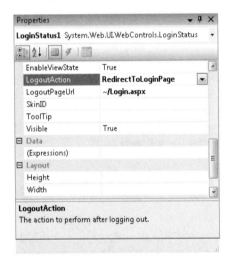

FIGURE 4-35 *LoginStatus* properties.

When you are finished configuring the *LoginStatus* server control, Default.aspx should look like Figure 4-36.

To see how these controls work, click **Run** on the standard toolbar to run the personal portal. Type in a valid user name and password. After a successful login, the default screen appears with both controls displaying.

As shown in Figure 4-37, the *LoginName* control displays my user name, "Eric", and, beside it, a link called Logout. (That is, because I am logged in, the only option available is to log out).

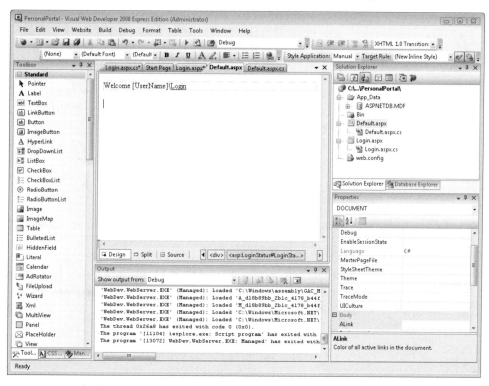

FIGURE 4-36 Default.aspx with *LoginName* and *LoginStatus* server controls.

FIGURE 4-37 Default.aspx with *LoginUser* and *LoginStatus* controls.

Click the **Logout** link, and you will be logged out and returned to the Login.aspx window. You can now log in again if you choose.

Changing User Passwords

Based on the requirements for your users, you know that you would like an easy way to change a password. Going directly to *ASPNETDB.MDF* is not recommended, and the ASP.NET

Configuration tool is not guaranteed to be available when you deploy the personal portal on a host.

Fortunately, ASP.NET has a server that enables users to change passwords.

Close the browser, if it's open, and return to Visual Web Developer. The first thing you must do is start grouping pages in folders to organize the site better. As a site grows and you add more functionality, it is important to start organizing related pages to make the site easier to understand and maintain. The functionality for changing passwords is an administration task, so create a new page called **ChangePassword** in a folder called **Admin**.

To add the ChangePassword page in a new site folder

1. Right-click the **PersonalPortal** project in **Solution Explorer**. Select **New Folder**.

2. Type **Admin** as the name of the folder.

3. Right-click the **Admin** folder and select **Add New Item**. In the **Add New Item** dialog box, select **Web Form** as the type of item and type **ChangePassword.aspx** as the name of the Web form.

> **Note** The URL for this page will be http://PersonalPortal:[PORTNUMBER]/Admin/
> ChangePassword.aspx.

Now you have a folder to store any pages that provide administrative functionality. As you build this site, you will group pages based on their functionality.

To add the ChangePassword server control to the ChangePassword.aspx page

1. Double-click the **ChangePassword.aspx** page in the **Admin** folder. In the **toolbox**, scroll down to the **Login** section.

2. Drag the **ChangePassword** server control to the outlined <div> element on the **ChangePassword.aspx** design surface. (See Figure 4-38.)

3. With the **ChangePassword** control selected, in the **Properties** window, change the **SuccessPageURL** property to **Default.aspx** by using the **Select URL** dialog box.

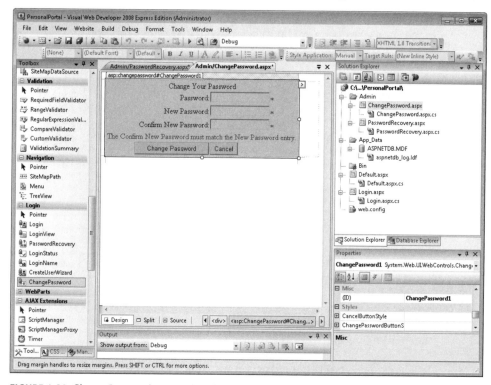

FIGURE 4-38 *ChangePassword* server control on ChangePassword.aspx.

Now that you have your Change Password page set up, the user has to have a way to open it. You must have a hyperlink to the ChangePassword.aspx page. Use the *HyperLink* server control.

To add a *HyperLink* server control to Default.aspx

1. Return to the **Default.aspx** screen by double-clicking it. Scroll up to the **Standard** section of the toolbox.

2. Select a hyperlink control and drag it underneath the **LoginName** and **LoginStatus** controls.

3. While the **HyperLink** control is selected, move to the **Properties** window.

4. Change the **Text** value in the **Appearance** section to **Change Password**.

5. Change the **NavigateURL** value, by using the **Select URL** dialog box in the **Navigation** section, to **ChangePassword.aspx**.

Run the personal portal by clicking **Run** on the standard toolbar. When the browser opens to the Login.aspx page, log in. When the browser opens the Default.aspx page, click the **Change Password** button. The ChangePassword.aspx page displays. (See Figure 4-39.)

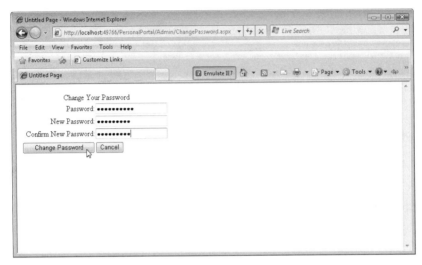

FIGURE 4-39 ChangePassword.aspx page.

Type your password in the *Password* field and type a new password in the *New Password* and *Confirm New Password* fields on the **ChangePassword.aspx** page. Click the **ChangePassword** button. If you filled out the fields correctly, you should be returned to the Default.aspx page with a new password.

Log out and try your new password.

Summary

In this chapter, you began work on the personal portal. You learned that using personas and stories is one way to define requirements for site development. You learned how to set up your site security and add new users. Looking under the hood, you discovered where ASP.NET stores its security data. Using ASP.NET built-in *Login* server controls, you added a Login page and a way for users to log out and change their password. Now that security is set up for the personal portal, you begin work in Chapter 5, "Using Master Pages," on a consistent look and feel across the site user master pages.

Chapter 5
Using Master Pages

After completing this chapter, you will be able to

- Create a master page.

- Understand *ContentPlaceHolder* controls.

- Understand *Content* controls.

- Attach a master page to an existing ASP.NET page.

- Create a nested master page.

In the previous chapter, you started creating the personal portal. In that chapter, I talked about organizing your pages in folders, which helps when your site grows in page count and functional complexity. It also helps you maintain the site.

In this chapter, you work with an ASP.NET technology called Master Pages. Master Pages enables you to centralize common markup and code and create a consistent look and feel across your site. Master Pages is a powerful technology of ASP.NET, but it can be very confusing. This chapter steps you through using Master Pages with your personal portal.

Creating a Master Page

Start Visual Web Developer and open the PersonalPortal project. Continuing the idea of folders for organization, create a folder by right-clicking the PersonalPortal project in Solution Explorer and select **New Folder**. Rename the folder to **MasterPages**.

To create a master page

1. Right-click the **MasterPages** folder in Solution Explorer. Select **Add New Item**.

2. When the Add New Item dialog box appears, select **Master Page** from the Templates list. (See Figure 5-1.)

3. Type **PersonalPortal.master** in the Name field.

4. Click the **Add** button to add PersonalPortal.master to the project.

FIGURE 5-1 Add New Item dialog box, adding a master page.

Content Placeholder Control

Double-click **PersonalPortal.master** in the MasterPages folder to open it in the Visual Web Developer editor. Select the **Source** view to see the markup. Listing 5-1 shows the markup of PersonalPortal.master. A lot of the markup looks like a regular ASP.NET Web form. In fact, it is identical to a new Web form except for one tag called <asp:ContentPlaceHolder> in two places, in the <head> and in the <div> in the <form> tag. What is this tag?

LISTING 5-1 PersonalPortal.Master

```
<%@ Master Language="C#" AutoEventWireup="true" CodeFile="PersonalPortal.master.cs"
Inherits="MasterPages_PersonalPortal" %>

<!DOCTYPE html PUBLIC "-//W3C//DTD XHTML 1.0 Transitional//EN" "http://www.w3.org/TR/xhtml1/
DTD/xhtml1-transitional.dtd">

<html xmlns="http://www.w3.org/1999/xhtml">
  <head runat="server">
    <title>Untitled Page</title>
    <asp:ContentPlaceHolder id="head" runat="server">

    </asp:ContentPlaceHolder>
  </head>

<body>
    <form id="form1" runat="server">

    <div>
```

```
    <asp:ContentPlaceHolder id="ContentPlaceHolder1" runat="server">

    </asp:ContentPlaceHolder>
  </div>

  </form>
</body>
</html>
```

The tag is for the *ContentPlaceHolder* control. It defines an area in the master page's Hypertext Markup Language (HTML) that renders all text, markup, and server controls from a related *Content* control found in a content page. (See Figure 5-2.)

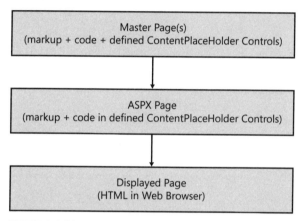

FIGURE 5-2 Master page to ASP.NET page to displayed page relationship.

A *Content* control is used in the ASPX page and associated with a *ContentPlaceHolder*, using its ContentPlaceHolderID property. Set the ContentPlaceHolderID property to the value of the ID property of the related *ContentPlaceHolder* control in a master page. More than one *ContentPlaceHolder* can be declared in a master page.

Select **Design** view in the editor and click the outline on the design surface to see the display illustrated in Figure 5-3.

FIGURE 5-3 *ContentPlaceHolder* control on design surface.

Within a page, only one *Content* control can supply the content for a *ContentPlaceHolder* on the master page. However, on each page that uses a master page, you can have separate *Content* controls associated with the *ContentPlaceHolder*. For example, you can define the *ContentPlaceHolder* for the page title in a master page. For each content page that uses the master page, you can add a *Content* control that supplies the text and markup for the page title.

Before you move on, change the contents of the <title> tags from Untitled Page to **My Personal Portal**. You'll see why as you keep reading.

Attaching a Master Page

Now that you have created a master page, the best way to understand it is to use it, so let's attach it to the Default.aspx page. Currently, the Default.aspx page's markup looks like Listing 5-2.

LISTING 5-2 Default.aspx Page

```
<%@ Page Language="C#" AutoEventWireup="true"  CodeFile="Default.aspx.cs" Inherits="_
Default" %>

<!DOCTYPE html PUBLIC "-//W3C//DTD XHTML 1.0 Transitional//EN" http://www.w3.org/TR/xhtml1/
DTD/xhtml1-transitional.dtd>

<html xmlns="http://www.w3.org/1999/xhtml">
<head runat="server">
    <title>My Personal Portal</title>
</head>
<body>
    <form id="form1" runat="server">
    <div>

        Welcome
        <asp:LoginName ID="LoginName1" runat="server" />
        !
        <asp:LoginStatus ID="LoginStatus1" runat="server" />

    </div>
    </form>
</body>
</html>
```

When you use a master page, it provides all the markup and code for the page that is common, so you don't have to have <html>, <head>, or <form> tags. The master page contains those tags, so if you don't have any content for your page, the markup will look like Listing 5-3. Remove all the markup except the first line of Default.aspx. (Don't worry; you add the *Login* and *LoginStatus* controls later.)

LISTING 5-3 Default.apx Page with no Markup

```
<%@ Page Language="C#" AutoEventWireup="true" CodeFile="Default.aspx.cs" Inherits="_Default"
%>
```

Now you have nothing on the page. Attach the PersonalPortal.master by typing the attribute master *MasterPageFile* between the *AutoEventWireup* and the *CodeFile* attributes. As you type, IntelliSense will help you finish typing. Enter the = sign to assign *MasterPageFile*, and IntelliSense lists the PersonalPortal.masterpage. (See Figure 5-4.)

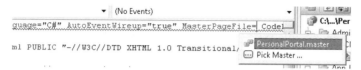

FIGURE 5-4 Add New Item dialog box, adding a master page.

Your markup should look like Listing 5-4.

LISTING 5-4 Default.aspx with a Master Page

```
<%@ Page Language="C#" AutoEventWireup="true" MasterPageFile="~/MasterPages/PersonalPortal.
master" CodeFile="Default.aspx.cs" Inherits="_Default" %>
```

Click **Run** from the standard toolbar. The Web browser opens to a blank personal portal page. (See Figure 5-5.) If you click **View** and select **Source**, you also see the HTML very similar to the blank Default.aspx page you created in Chapter 4, "Creating Your First Web Site."

FIGURE 5-5 Default.aspx with PersonalPortal.master.

The PersonalPortal master page supplied all the HTML for the page, so if you add more HTML or code to the PersonalPortal.master, any page that uses it will have that markup and code added to it automatically.

So what if you want markup or code to appear only on the page itself and not on every page? You use the *ContentPlaceHolder* control on the master page to determine where the markup will be placed and the *Content* control on the page to place the markup and code specific to that page. Listing 5-1 of PersonalPortal.master shows that the controls are located in the <head> tag and the <div> tag of the form. Markup in pages that use the PersonalPortal master page have these two locations to add content.

The following example shows a <asp:Content> tag not a <asp:ContentPlaceHolder> tag.

Go back to Default.aspx and add a <asp:Content> tag in the page, with the text **I love Visual Web Developer!**. Default.aspx should look like Listing 5-5. (See Figure 5-6.)

LISTING 5-5 Default.aspx

```
<%@ Page Language="C#" AutoEventWireup="true" MasterPageFile="~/MasterPages/PersonalPortal.
master" CodeFile="Default.aspx.cs" Inherits="_Default" %>

<asp:Content ID="SomeContent" ContentPlaceHolderID="ContentPlaceHolder1" runat="server" >
  I Love Visual Web Developer!
</asp:Content>
```

FIGURE 5-6 Default.aspx with a *Content* control.

Creating a Look and Feel

In Chapter 4, I talked about how the Eric persona used a variety of Internet sites and services while he was traveling. The big problem was that the functionality he used was divided in different Web sites. The personal portal will bring those features together in one interface.

When you are designing the look and feel of a site, a great way to visualize it is by using wireframes. Wireframes are a basic way of displaying the design of a Web page. You can draw it on a sheet of paper or with a drawing program such as Microsoft Paint or diagramming software such as Microsoft Office Visio.

Figure 5-7 shows a wireframe of the home page of the personal portal.

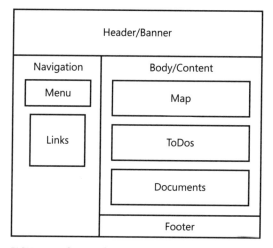

FIGURE 5-7 Personal portal Default.aspx page design.

- **Header/Banner**   The Header/Banner area will have an image and contain the title of the site.

- **Navigation**   The Navigation area will have the *Login* and *Login Status* controls, a menu to reach the different pages in the site, and an area for links.

- **Map**   The Map section of the page will contain the Microsoft Virtual Earth map and some way to control it.

- **ToDo**   The ToDo area will contain a list of the to-dos.

- **Documents**   The Documents area will show the list of documents that have been uploaded to the site and will have some controls to help upload files.

Designing the Personal Portal Master Page

Now that you have a basic design of the site, you design what will be on the personal portal master page. Typically, the common areas of a Web site are Header/Banner, Navigation, and Footer. The Body/Content area is where the page's unique content is displayed.

Based on what you know about master pages, you design the page layout and then place *ContentPlaceHolder* controls in the regions you reserve for a corresponding *Content* control on a page. That would mean one *Content ControlPlaceHolder* control for the Body/Content area of your design.

First, let's define the layout by using a table.

> **Note** For you advanced users who prefer to use <div> and cascading style sheets (CSS), bear with me. Using HTML tables might be old fashioned, but it's more straightforward for new designers. Chapter 7, "Working with HTML and JavaScript," begins using CSS extensively.

Visual Web Developer has HTML table creation functionality available through the Table menu. Because it generates markup that uses some advanced features of CSS, you type in the HTML markup in directly.

To add a table for the layout

1. Double-click **PersonalPortal.master** in Solution Explorer. Make sure you are in Design view.

2. Click in the <div> outline of the PersonalPortal.master.

3. From the Table menu, select **Insert Table**.

   The Insert Table dialog box appears. (See Figure 5-8.)

4. Enter **3** for the number of rows and leave the number of columns at the default value of 2.

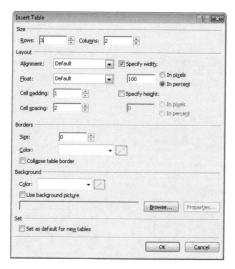

FIGURE 5-8 Insert Table dialog box.

5. Click **OK** to create the table.

   Figure 5-9 illustrates the new table, but it doesn't look like the drawing of the layout you designed. You must create the Header and Navigation areas.

FIGURE 5-9 The newly inserted table.

You can create them by merging the cells in the top row and the cells in the left column.

To merge the cells in a table

1. Select the top two cells by dragging the mouse across them.

   Figure 5-10 shows the top two cells selected.

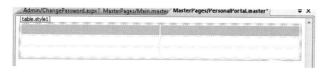

FIGURE 5-10 Top selected cells.

2. Right-click either of the cells. From the pop-up, select **Modify**, and then choose **Merge Cells**.

FIGURE 5-11 Merging cells in a table.

3. Select the left two cells to the right of the table in the last two rows and right-click **Modify**. Choose **Merge Cells**.

The finished table should look like Figure 5-12.

FIGURE 5-12 Final table on design surface.

The code in Listing 5-6 shows you the markup that Visual Web Developer added to PersonalPortal.master.

LISTING 5-6 PersonalPortal.master with Table

```
<%@ Master Language="C#" AutoEventWireup="true" CodeFile="PersonalPortal.master.cs"
Inherits="PersonalPortal" %>

<!DOCTYPE html PUBLIC "-//W3C//DTD XHTML 1.0 Transitional//EN" http://www.w3.org/TR/xhtml1/
DTD/xhtml1-transitional.dtd>

<html xmlns="http://www.w3.org/1999/xhtml">
<head runat="server">
    <title>My Personal Portal</title>
```

```
        <asp:ContentPlaceHolder id="head" runat="server">
        </asp:ContentPlaceHolder>
        <style type="text/css">
            .style1
            {
                width: 100%;
            }
        </style>
    </head>
    <body>

        <form id="form1" runat="server">
        <div>
            <table class="style1">
                <tr>
                    <td colspan="2">
                         </td>
                </tr>
                <tr>
                    <td rowspan="2">
                         </td>
                    <td>
                         </td>
                </tr>
                <tr>
                    <td>
                         </td>
                </tr>
            </table>
        </div>
        </form>
    </body>
    </html>
```

You will notice that there are style attributes for <td> and <tr> tags and the <style> tag in the header. This is CSS markup that gives you greater control of HTML. I won't explore CSS here; Chapter 11, "Understanding and Using Mashups," goes into detail about it.

Adding the *Login* and *LoginStatus* Controls

Let's add the *Login* and *LoginStatus* controls back into the Navigation area of the table. Open the toolbox and drag and drop the *Login* and then the *LoginStatus* controls from the Security section of the toolbox, as you did in Chapter 4, into the Navigation section of the table. When you are finished, the PersonalPortal.master should look like Figure 5-13.

To see what your changes look like in the browser, click **Run** from the standard toolbar. After you log in, the Default.aspx page display should look like Figure 5-14.

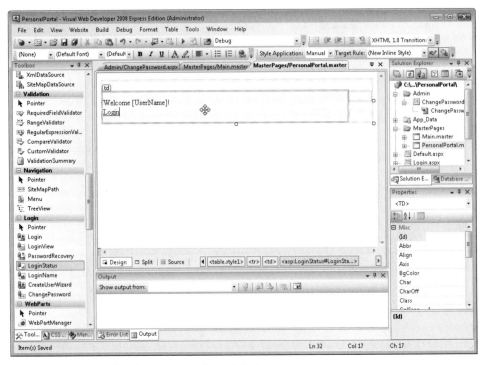

FIGURE 5-13 *Login* and *LoginStatus* controls on Default.aspx.

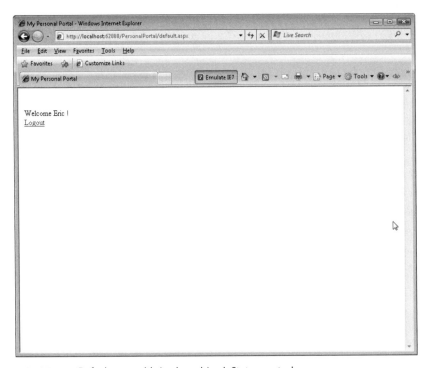

FIGURE 5-14 Default.aspx with *Login* and *LoginStatus* controls.

Adding a *ContentPlaceHolder*

Going back to your design (shown in Figure 5-7), you know that you need the Map, ToDo and Document functionalities to appear in the Body/Content area. These are represented by the cell in the right-side column in the second row. You know that this area must be defined in the master page and filled in the page using it. In this case, you need to create a *ContentPlaceHolder* control in the cell in the PersonalPortal.master, and a *Content* control will be used in Default.aspx to fill it.

Name the control **PersonalPortalContent**. Add the following markup to the cell in the table:

```
<asp:ContentPlaceHolder ID="PersonalPortalContent" runat="server" />
```

This is the markup for a *ContentPlaceHolder* control. The name of the area to be referenced later in Default.aspx is assigned using the *ID* attribute.

Adding this markup to the cell makes the cell visible in the designer, as Figure 5-15 shows.

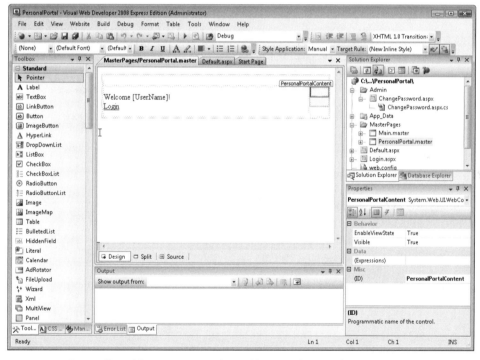

FIGURE 5-15 PersonalPortalContent *ContentPlaceHolderControl* selected in the designer.

To be clear about what is happening, Figure 5-16 shows the relationships that develop.

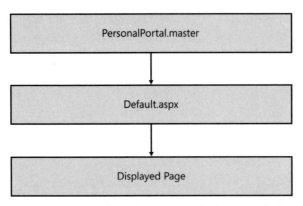

FIGURE 5-16 PersonalPortal.master to Default.aspx to displayed page relationship.

Double-click **Default.aspx** in Solution Explorer to open it. Select the code view and type the markup to match the code in Listing 5-7.

LISTING 5-7 DEFAULT.ASPX

```
<%@ Master Language="C#" MasterPageFile="~/PersonalPortal.master" AutoEventWireup="false"
CodeFile="Default.aspx.cs" Inherits="Main" %>

<asp:Content ID="Content1" ContentPlaceHolderID="head" Runat="Server">

</asp:Content>
<asp:Content ID="Content2" ContentPlaceHolderID="PersonalPortalContent" Runat="Server">

I Love Visual Web Developer!

</asp:Content>
```

You typed **I Love Visual Web Developer!** into the *Content* control for PersonalPortalContent. To see the result, click **Run** from the standard toolbar. After you log in, Default.aspx looks like Figure 5-17.

FIGURE 5-17 Default.aspx with a *Content* control, displaying text.

Creating a Nested Master Page

You've created your master page to be used on all pages. However, you also must define the area for the map, to-dos, and documents. You use a powerful capability of master pages: the ability to nest master pages. Figure 5-18 shows how this works.

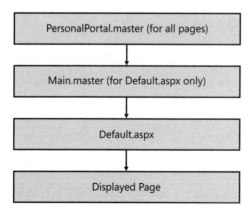

FIGURE 5-18 Nested Main.master master page.

The PersonalPortal master page will still define the Header, Navigation, and Footer areas. The Main master page will use the PersonalPortal.master file as a parent master page; it will be for the Default.aspx page only, and it will define the body and content areas for the Map, ToDo, and Document areas.

To create a nested master page

1. Right-click the **MasterPages** folder in Solution Explorer.

2. Select **Add New Item**.

3. When the Add New Item dialog box appears, select **Master Page** from the Templates list and type **Main.master** in the Name field. (See Figure 5-19.)

FIGURE 5-19 Creating Main.master in the Add New Item dialog box.

4. Select the **Select Master Page** check box. Click the **Add** button.

   The **Select a Master Page** dialog appears.

5. Select **PersonalPortal.master** from the MasterPages folder. Click the **OK** button.

After Main.master is created in the MasterPages folder, double-click it and select the Source view in the editor. You know from your design in Figure 5-7 that you want content areas for maps, to-dos, and documents. For each one, create a *ContentPlaceHolder* control and put a label above each control to indicate what it is for. Your markup should match Listing 5-8.

LISTING 5-8 Main.master

```
<%@ Master Language="C#" MasterPageFile="~/MasterPages/PersonalPortal.master"
AutoEventWireup="false" CodeFile="Main.master.cs" Inherits="Main" %>
```

```
<asp:Content ID="Content1" ContentPlaceHolderID="head" Runat="Server">

</asp:Content>

<asp:Content ID="Content2" ContentPlaceHolderID="PersonalPortalContent" Runat="Server">
    <div>
    <div >My Maps</div>
    <asp:contentplaceholder id="MyMapContent" runat="server"/>
    <div>My Todo List</div>
    <asp:contentplaceholder id="MyTodoContent" runat="server"/>
    <div>My Documents</div>
    <asp:contentplaceholder id="MyDocumentsContent" runat="server"/>
</div>
</asp:Content>
```

Notice how the *MasterPageFile* attribute was set by the dialog box when you created the master page. Notice also that the <div> tag was used to wrap around the labels and all the contents in the *PersonalPortalContent Content* control. You will understand the reason behind using the <div> tags in Chapter 10, "Using Cascading Style Sheets to Change the Look and Feel of Pages," about style sheets.

Switch to the Design view in the Visual Web Developer editor, shown in Figure 5-20, to see what it looks like.

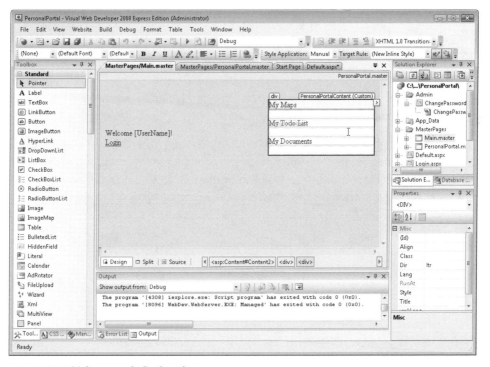

FIGURE 5-20 Main.master in Design view.

To see the result, click **Run** from the standard toolbar. After you log in, Default.aspx looks like Figure 5-21.

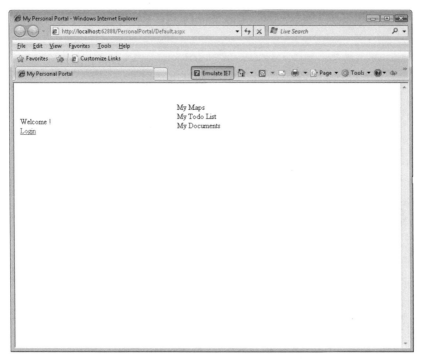

FIGURE 5-21 Default.aspx with nested master page Main.master.

I know I promised to show you how to do everything step by step. I have to this point. I want to give you an opportunity to try it by yourself.

Your assignment: Attach the PersonalPortal.master file to the ChangePassword.aspx page in the Admin folder. Follow the similar steps shown earlier in this chapter and see whether you can get ChangePassword.aspx to look like Figure 5-22 in Visual Web Developer. You can always check out the code for this chapter in the accompanying CD to see if you have it right.

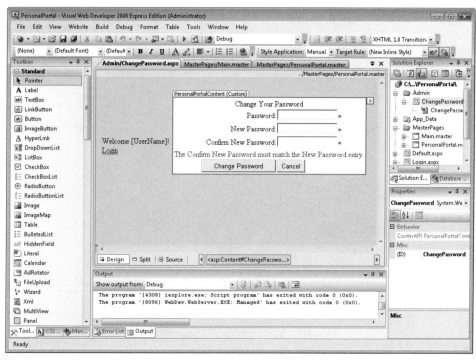

FIGURE 5-22 ChangePassword.aspx with PersonalPortal.master in Design view.

Summary

In this chapter, you learned how to use Master Pages to create reusable markup and provide a consistent look and feel for your site. In the next chapter, you continue to add functionality to the personal portal with server controls in Visual Web Developer.

Chapter 6
Using Server Controls

After completing this chapter, you will be able to

- Create a server control.

- Set server control properties in the Properties window.

- Set server control properties with markup in the editor.

- Set server control properties visually in the editor.

- Use multiple server controls together.

- Create a menu for site navigations.

In the preceding chapter, you designed the layout of the personal portal. With master pages, you learned how to reuse markup and code in ASP.NET Web pages for a consistent look and feel. Another important reusable technology in ASP.NET is server controls. You began to use server controls in Chapter 4, "Creating Your First Web Site." You created the *Login* and *LoginStatus* server controls and used them with your personal portal security.

In this chapter, you explore a few more server controls to add more functionality to the personal portal.

Visual Web Developer Server Controls

The Toolbox contains all the controls you use when you create ASP.NET pages. Figure 6-1 shows all the categories of controls.

FIGURE 6-1 The Toolbox control categories.

- **Standard**   The controls in the standard category contain *Button*, *Listbox*, *Hyperlink*, and *Label* as well as controls such as *Image*, *Table*, *Calendar*, and *ImageMaps*.

- **Data**   These controls are unique to ASP.NET and ADO (Active Data Objects).NET. They connect to and display information from sources of data such as databases and formatted files such as XML documents. Chapter 8, "Working with Databases," covers databases in greater detail. In this chapter, you use one data source, called *SiteMapDataSource*.

- **Validation**   Validation server controls are a collection of controls that enable you to validate an associated input server control, such as *TextBox*, and display a custom message when validation fails. Each validation control performs a specific type of validation.

- **Navigation**   In this section are controls to create menus and other navigation aids on ASP.NET Web pages.

- **Login**   You used two of these controls in Chapter 4: *Login* and *LoginStatus*. This section also includes controls that enable you to build a login page, enable users to register on your Web site, and display different information to logged-in and anonymous users.

- **WebParts**   This section contains the ASP.NET server controls you can use to display Web parts on a Web page.

- **AJAX Extensions**   Asynchronous JavaScript and XML (AJAX) is a group of interrelated Web development techniques used for creating interactive Web applications. This new Web development technology extends ASP.NET, offering the interactive user interface benefits of AJAX with a programming model that is more familiar to ASP.NET developers, making it very easy to add AJAX to your applications quickly and with minimal effort.

- **HTML**   By default, HTML elements on an ASP.NET Web page are not available to the server; they are treated as text that is passed through to the browser. However, with HTML server controls, they are exposed as elements you can program in server-based code.

Adding a *Label* Server Control

Start working with server controls by adding a copyright notice in the footer of the personal portal; you can use a label in this area. Based on your design of the personal portal layout, you must add to the footer defined by the table of the PersonalPortal.master.

Open Visual Web Developer and the personal portal project. Double-click the **PersonalPortal.master** in **Solution Explorer** to show its markup. Listing 6-1 shows the markup from your work in the previous chapter.

LISTING 6-1 PERSONALPORTAL.MASTER

```
<%@ Master Language="C#" AutoEventWireup="true" CodeFile="PersonalPortal.master.cs"
Inherits="PersonalPortal" %>
```

```
<!DOCTYPE html PUBLIC "-//W3C//DTD XHTML 1.0 Transitional//EN" "http://www.w3.org/TR/xhtml1/
DTD/xhtml1-transitional.dtd">

<html xmlns="http://www.w3.org/1999/xhtml">
<head runat="server">
    <title>My Personal Portal</title>
    <asp:ContentPlaceHolder id="head" runat="server">
    </asp:ContentPlaceHolder>
    <style type="text/css">
        .style1
        {
            width: 100%;
        }
    </style>
</head>
<body>
    <form id="form1" runat="server">
    <div>

        <table class="style1">
            <tr>
                <td colspan="2">
                     </td>
            </tr>
            <tr>
                <td rowspan="2">
                    Welcome
                    <asp:LoginName ID="LoginName1" runat="server" />
                    !<br />
                    <asp:LoginStatus ID="LoginStatus1" runat="server" />
                </td>
                <td>
                    <asp:ContentPlaceHolder ID="PersonalPortalContent" runat="server" >

                    </asp:ContentPlaceHolder>
                     
                </td>
            </tr>
            <tr>
                <td>
                     </td>
            </tr>
        </table>

    </div>
    </form>
</body>
</html>
```

The markup shows the *Login* and *LoginStatus* controls you use for the site's security.

Set the editor to Design and to view the PersonalPortal.master. Open the Toolbar if it is not displayed and drag **Label** from the Standard section to the footer location in the table. (See Figure 6-2.)

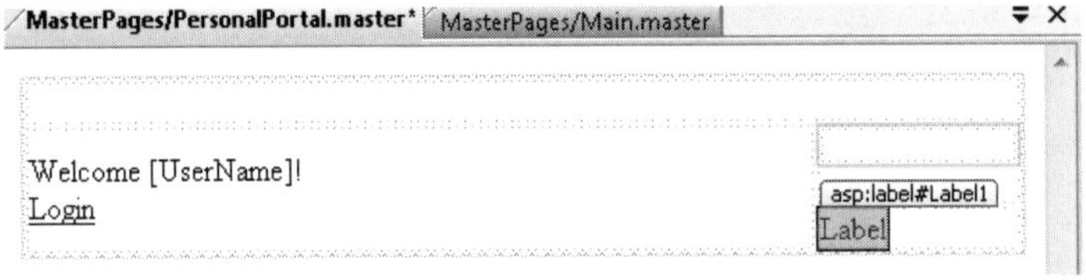

FIGURE 6-2 Label in the footer.

Select the control and look at the Properties window. Scroll up and down to see the various properties you can change. Clicking inside the cell to the right of the property name enables you to set the value. Also notice that a help tip appears in the area below the properties. Click the right column next to the Text property. Type **@Copyright 2009** <***Your Name Here***>. (See Figure 6-3).

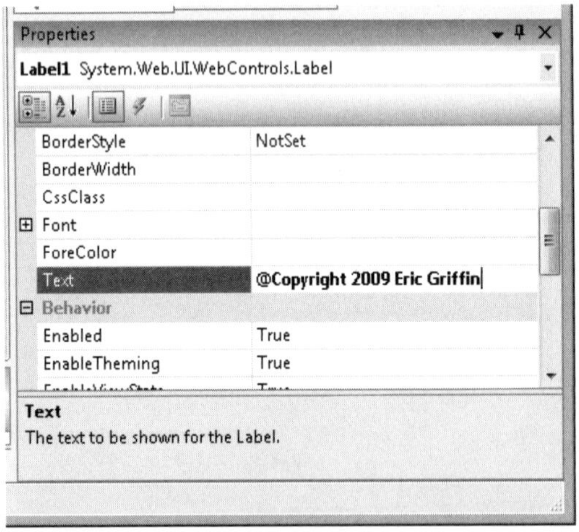

FIGURE 6-3 Text property for the copyright label.

Return to the editor and switch to the Source view of PersonalPortal.master. You can see the markup has been added to the footer location in the table.

```
<asp:Label ID="Label1" runat="server" Text="@Copyright 2009 Eric Griffin"></asp:Label>
```

You can also see that the value you entered for the Text property has been entered for you as an attribute. Visual Web Developer handles this interaction, constantly syncronizing with your markup the changes you make in the Properties window.

You can also type property values in directly. Place the cursor behind the *runat="server"* attribute and press the space bar. IntelliSense will display a pop-up menu with all the properties that appeared in the Properties window. Selecting the property inserts the property into the markup as an attribute. (See Figure 6-4.)

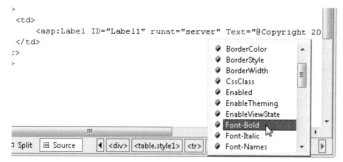

FIGURE 6-4 Using IntelliSense to set properties.

To see the results of your work, click **Run** on the standard toolbar. The browser window will display as illustrated in Figure 6-5.

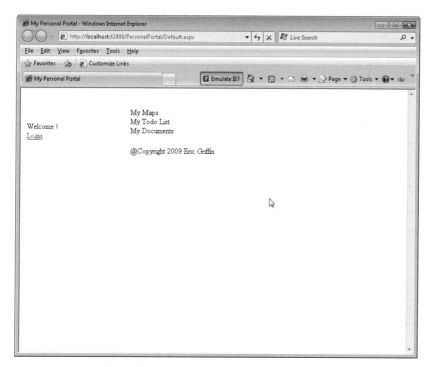

FIGURE 6-5 Personal portal with *Label* server control.

Adding Navigation Server Controls

The *Label* server control is a simple one. It is independent and doesn't rely on other server controls to function.

Based on the requirements defined in Chapter 4, you know that the personal portal will have many areas of functionality. The user of the site, Eric, will need a way to navigate to that functionality. Usually, that is done with a menu. The Navigation section of controls has a *Menu* server control to use. Although this control can be used alone, like the label, it works better with supporting controls. These supporting controls can make it easier for you to maintain your site after it is running. By using the *SiteMapDataSource* with the *Menu* control, you can configure the *Menu* control dynamically without returning to Visual Web Developer after you have deployed your site.

Before you can create the *Menu* control, you need a *SiteMapDataSource* for it to work with. As implied by its name, the *SiteMapDataSouce* requires a SiteMap data file.

To create the SiteMap data file

1. Right-click the **PersonalPortal** project in Solution Explorer and select **Add New Item**. (See Figure 6-6.)

FIGURE 6-6 Creating a site map, using Add New Item.

2. Select **SiteMap** from the **Templates** list and type **web.sitemap** in the name field.

   The web.sitemap file will be in the root of the PersonalPortal project directory structure. (See Figure 6-7.)

3. Double-click the **web.sitemap** file to open it in the editor.

FIGURE 6-7 The web.sitemap file in Solution Explorer.

The web.sitemap file is an XML file. (See Listing 6-2.)

LISTING 6-2 New web.sitemap

```
<?xml version="1.0" encoding="utf-8" ?>
<siteMap xmlns="http://schemas.microsoft.com/AspNet/SiteMap-File-1.0" >
    <siteMapNode url="" title=""  description="">
        <siteMapNode url="" title=""  description="" />
        <siteMapNode url="" title=""  description="" />
    </siteMapNode>
</siteMap>
```

The *siteMapNode* element with the *url*, *title*, and *description* attributes defines the menu and menu item. Nesting a *siteMapNode* within another defines a submenu. Type the markup until web.sitemap looks like Listing 6-3.

LISTING 6-3 Modified web.sitemap

```
<?xml version="1.0" encoding="utf-8" ?>
<siteMap xmlns="http://schemas.microsoft.com/AspNet/SiteMap-File-1.0" >
  <siteMapNode url="~/Default.aspx" title="Home"  description="">
        <siteMapNode url="~/Admin/ChangePassword.aspx" title="Change Password"
description="Change Your Password" />
    </siteMapNode>
</siteMap>
```

The first *siteMapNode* defines the top level, titled Home, whose URL is defined as "~/Default. aspx". The "~" is a shortcut for the root of the site. The single nested *siteMapNode* with the title of "Change Password" has a URL defined or "~/Admin/ChangePassword.aspx". This is pointing to the ChangePassword.aspx page in the Admin folder of the site.

Any time you must add a new menu item to point to a page on your site, go to this XML file and edit it.

Creating a *SiteMapDataSource* Control

Now that you have created the web.sitemap XML file to be used for your menu, you need a mechanism to connect to it. For this, you use a new type of control that does not have a visible interface. It is a server control called *SiteMapDataSource*. *Data Source* server controls connect to databases or files. *SiteMapDataSource* is built to connect to site map data files.

To create a *SiteMapDataSource* server control, make sure the editor is in Design view on the personal portal master page. (Because you want this to appear on all pages, this is the best place to put it.)

Drag a *SiteMapDataSource* control from the Data section of the Toolbox to the bottom portion of the PersonalPortal.master. (See Figure 6-8.)

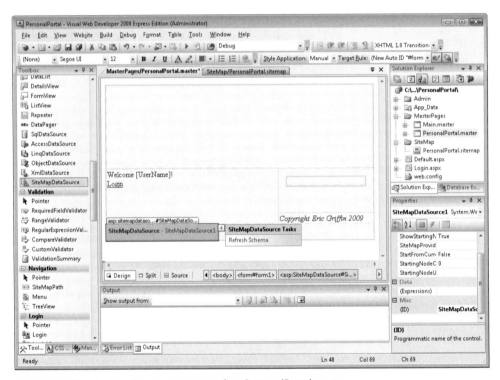

FIGURE 6-8 *SiteMapDataSource* server control on PersonalPortal.master.

The *SiteMapDataSource* control connects to web.sitemap by default, but it is not a visual control. If you run the personal portal, you will see no visible change to the site. To tap into the data it is managing, you need to connect to visual control.

Under the **Navigation** section in the Toolbox, drag a *Menu* server control to below the *LoginStatus* server control on PersonalPortal.master. (See Figure 6-9.)

FIGURE 6-9 *Menu* server control on PersonalPortal.master.

By default, the *Menu* server control is not connected to any data source. You can type in the menus and menu items manually by editing the Items property in the Properties window. Click the ellipses to open the Menu Item editor dialog box. (See Figure 6-10.) Doing it this way, the menu items will be fixed and static after you deploy your site. The only way to update it would be to rebuild the site and redeploy it.

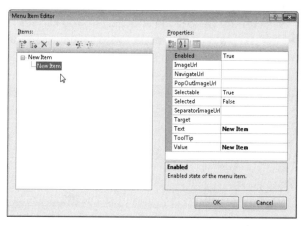

FIGURE 6-10 *Menu* server control on PersonalPortal.master.

However, there's a better way to populate the menu, using a sitemap file and a *SiteMapDataSource* control, but you must connect the menu to it. Click the **Menu** server control to activate it. Then click the arrow in the upper left corner to open a pop-up menu. (See Figure 6-11.)

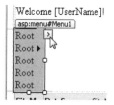

FIGURE 6-11 Selecting the Menu arrow.

The pop-up menu gives you a drop-down menu from which to choose a data source. By clicking the drop-down menu, you see the *SiteMapDataSource* control you added on the list, as shown in Figure 6-12. Select it.

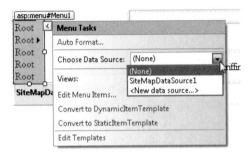

FIGURE 6-12 Selecting the data source.

After the data source is set, the *Menu* control will change appearance. You can see that the top-level menu you defined as Home is showing in the Visual Web Developer editor. (See Figure 6-13.)

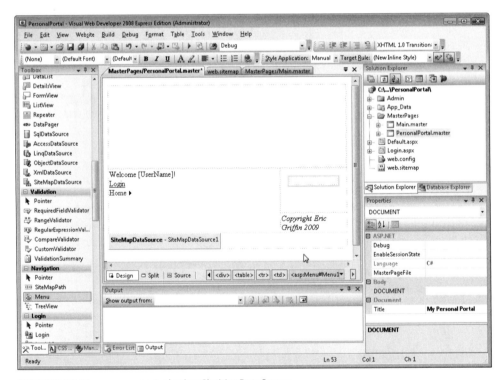

FIGURE 6-13 *Menu* server control using *SiteMapDataSource*.

To see what your menu looks like, click **Run** on the standard toolbar. After you log in, you will see a screen that looks like Figure 6-14. Click the arrow next to the Home menu to see Change Password. Select it to access the ChangePassword.aspx page.

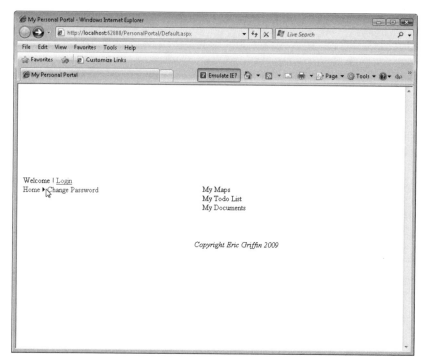

FIGURE 6-14 Home menu showing Change Password.

Summary

In this chapter, you learned how to use a few of the dozens of server controls available to you in Visual Web Developer and ASP.NET. You learned how to set their properties visually, in the Properties window, or directly in the editor, with markup. Server controls can work together to give you greater flexibility and maintainability. Feel free to experiment with more of the server controls. You will use more of them in later chapters of this book.

Chapter 7
Working with HTML and JavaScript

After completing this chapter, you will be able to

- Embed a Virtual Earth Map Control in an ASP.NET page.

- Create JavaScript functions in an ASP.NET page.

- Create a user interface to manipulate the Virtual Earth map control dynamically.

- Configure Internet Explorer for JavaScript debugging.

- Configure Visual Web Developer for JavaScript debugging.

- Enable debugging in Internet Explorer.

- Set a breakpoint in JavaScript code.

- Inspect JavaScript variable values during debugging.

- Change values of JavaScript variables while debugging.

In this chapter, you build more into the personal portal. In Chapter 4, "Creating Your First Web Site," your persona, Eric, uses maps as he travels to find places to eat and directions to them, so he needs the ability to use a map in the portal.

You will use the Hypertext Markup Language (HTML) and JavaScript editing capabilities of Visual Web Developer. JavaScript is an important Web language used to create dynamic sites; you'll use it to integrate Microsoft Virtual Earth into the personal portal.

Introducing Virtual Earth

If you have used the Internet to find a business or person and then get directions on how to get there, you probably used a map. Virtual Earth is a Microsoft technology that is built into the Live search engine. The Live search engine is available at *http://maps.live.com* or from the MSN home page at *http://www.msn.com*. Figure 7-1 shows the Live Search Maps Web site.

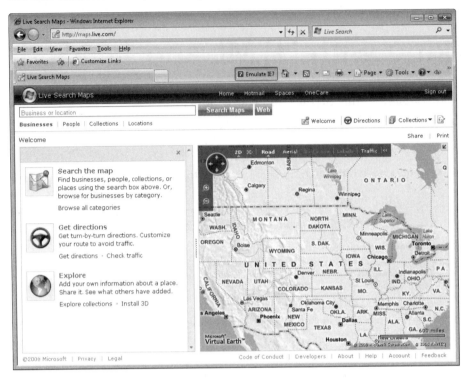

FIGURE 7-1 Live Search Maps.

The map to the right of the screen shot is the *Virtual Earth* control. Because it is a control, it is reusable, but it is not a server control available in Visual Web Developer. However, you can integrate it into your ASP.NET pages by using HTML and JavaScript.

Microsoft offers complete documentation with examples on how to use the *Virtual Earth* control at *http://dev.live.com/virtualearth/sdk/.* The Web site is called the Virtual Earth Interactive SDK (software development kit); it shows you the control working in a Web site and then shows the code that created it. Figure 7-2 shows the site.

I won't regurgitate documentation you can easily read on your own. I want you to learn by doing and then expand on what you build in the personal portal.

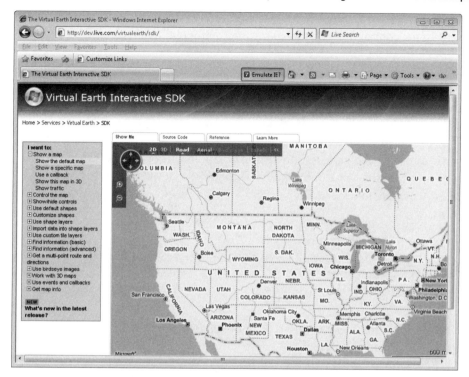

FIGURE 7-2 Virtual Earth Interactive SDK.

Integrating Virtual Earth into the Personal Portal

To integrate Virtual Earth, you have to use JavaScript and HTML. The *Virtual Earth* control needs to reference a JavaScript library before you can use it. Use the following code to reference it on your page:

```
<script type="text/javascript"
src="http://dev.virtualearth.net/mapcontrol/mapcontrol.ashx?v=6"></script>
```

The next decision is where to place it. You know from your layout design in Chapter 4 that the control will appear on the main site. This means that the HTML markup will likely appear in the *Content* control of the Main.master file. Because the Virtual Earth JavaScript library needs to be available when the markup in Main.master is displayed, you must place the library reference in the parent master page: PersonalPortal.master. Also, PersonalPortal. master contains the <head> tag for the personal portal HTML. This is where the <script> tag must go.

In **PersonalPortal.master** in the Visual Web Developer editor's **Source view**, type the text for the <script> tag below the <style> tag used for the table. (See Listing 7-1.)

Now that you have a Virtual Earth JavaScript library referenced, you can add JavaScript code to create the control. The code to create the control is as follows:

```
var map = null;
function GetMap()
{
    map = new VEMap('myMap');
    map.LoadMap(null, 10 ,'h' ,false);
}
```

The *GetMap()* function creates the *VEMap* object and sends the *myMap* parameter. You'll use this later for the name of the *<div>* placeholder that will display the *Virtual Earth* control. (You'll create this soon.) The next line calls the control's *LoadMap* function to display the control.

> **Note** You can read more about the *GetMap* constructor and the *LoadMap* function at *http://msdn.microsoft.com/library/bb412544.aspx* and *http://msdn.microsoft.com/library/bb412546.aspx*, respectively.

This code needs to be in its own <script> tag underneath the *Virtual Earth* control <script> tag you just added. (See Listing 7-1.)

LISTING 7-1 <HEAD> TAG OF PERSONALPORTAL.MASTER

```
<head runat="server">
    <title>My Personal Portal</title>
    <asp:ContentPlaceHolder id="head" runat="server">
    </asp:ContentPlaceHolder>
    <style type="text/css">

        .style1
        {
            width: 100%;
        }
    </style>

    <script type="text/javascript" src="http://dev.virtualearth.net/mapcontrol/mapcontrol.
ashx?v=6"></script>

    <script type="text/javascript">
        var map = null;
        function GetMap()
        {
            map = new VEMap('myMap');
            map.LoadMap(null, 10 ,'h' ,false);
        }

    </script>
</head>
```

You're almost there. You have two more things to do. First, it is great that the library is referenced for the *GetMap* function to create the *Virtual Earth* control. However, if you ran the project right now, nothing would happen. You must add a place for the control to display and call the *GetMap* function through an event when the page is displayed. JavaScript is hooked into HTML page events to allow for functions such as *GetMap* to be called. Here is the code you must add to the <body> tag on the PersonalPortal.master HTML:

```
<body onload="GetMap();">
```

The *onload* attribute signals the browser to execute the text, when the page is loading, as a JavaScript statement. In this case, the GetMap(); statement is executed.

You have added everything you need to load the *Virtual Earth* control. Listing 7-2 shows PersonalPortal.master with all the changes.

LISTING 7-2 PERSONALPORTAL.MASTER WITH GETMAP FUNCTION

```
<%@ Master Language="C#" AutoEventWireup="true" CodeFile="PersonalPortal.master.cs"
Inherits="PersonalPortal" %>

<!DOCTYPE html PUBLIC "-//W3C//DTD XHTML 1.0 Transitional//EN" "http://www.w3.org/TR/xhtml1/
DTD/xhtml1-transitional.dtd">

<html xmlns="http://www.w3.org/1999/xhtml">

<head runat="server">
    <title>My Personal Portal</title>
    <asp:ContentPlaceHolder id="head" runat="server">
    </asp:ContentPlaceHolder>
    <style type="text/css">

        .style1
        {
            width: 100%;
        }
    </style>

    <script type="text/javascript" src="http://dev.virtualearth.net/mapcontrol/mapcontrol.
ashx?v=6"></script>

    <script type="text/javascript">
        var map = null;
        function GetMap()
        {
            map = new VEMap('myMap');
            map.LoadMap(null, 10 ,'h' ,false);
        }

    </script>
</head>
<body onload="GetMap();">
    <form id="form1" runat="server">
    <div>
```

```
<table class="style1">
    <tr>
        <td colspan="2">
             </td>
    </tr>
    <tr>
        <td rowspan="2">
            Welcome
            <asp:LoginName ID="LoginName1" runat="server" />
            !<br />
            <asp:LoginStatus ID="LoginStatus1" runat="server" />
            <asp:Menu ID="Menu1" runat="server"
DataSourceID="SiteMapDataSource1">
            </asp:Menu>
        </td>
        <td>
            <asp:ContentPlaceHolder ID="PersonalPortalContent" runat="server" >

            </asp:ContentPlaceHolder>
             
        </td>
    </tr>
    <tr>
        <td>
            <asp:Label ID="Label1" runat="server" Text="@Copyright 2009 Eric
Griffin"></asp:Label>
        </td>
    </tr>
</table>

</div>
<asp:SiteMapDataSource ID="SiteMapDataSource1" runat="server" />
</form>
</body>
</html>
```

Now you add the display area for Virtual Earth Map Control. You know that the Virtual
Earth map should appear in the content area of the Default.aspx file. To display content
on this page—because it is inheriting markup from Main.master—you must place it in a
Content display control. In Main.master, you defined a *ContentPlaceHolder* control with
the MyMapContent ID. Now, in Default.aspx, you must add a *Content* server control with a
ContentPlaceHolderID of *MyMapContent*. Listing 7-3 shows the how the markup should look.

LISTING 7-3 DEFAULT.ASPX WITH VIRTUAL EARTH <DIV> PLACEHOLDER

```
<%@ Page Language="C#" AutoEventWireup="true" MasterPageFile="~/MasterPages/Main.master"
CodeFile="Default.aspx.cs" Inherits="_Default" %>

<asp:Content ID="Content1" ContentPlaceHolderID="MyMapContent" runat="server" >

    <div id='myMap' style="position:relative; width:600px; height:400px;" ></div>

</asp:Content>
```

A *<div>* placeholder is in this *Content* display control. It has an ID of myMap. It is the same name you used in the *GetMap* JavaScript function in Listing 7-1. The Virtual Earth JavaScript library will use this *<div>* as a placeholder for the positioning and size of the control. A style attribute defines the position, the width, and the height.

You can see the *<div>* placeholder in the Design view of Visual Web Developer, as is shown in Figure 7-3.

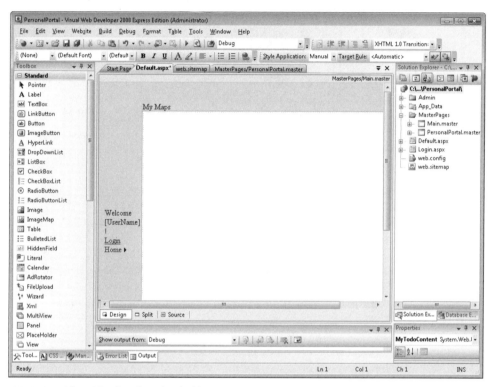

FIGURE 7-3 Virtual Earth *<div>* placeholder.

You have added everything you need to display the *Virtual Earth* control. Let's see Virtual Earth in action.

Press **Run** from the standard toolbar. The personal portal will open in the browser to display the image illustrated in Figure 7-4.

The *Virtual Earth* control appears in the exact location of the *<div>* placeholder. The map is in the default location. You have all the default menu controls and can drag the map around as if it were on the Live Search Maps page.

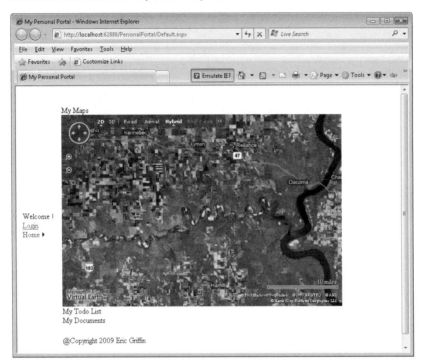

FIGURE 7-4 The *Virtual Earth* control running in the personal portal.

This is great but not as useful as it could be. This is supposed to be a personal site, so let's make it more personal by selecting a new default location for the map. Let's say your user Eric lives in Atlanta. It would be great if the map could open, by default, to the city of Atlanta, Georgia.

Return to the Virtual Earth SDK. If you examine the methods and functions the control has, you will see a function you can use to set the location of the map. It's no surprise that it is named *Find*. You can read the documentation for it at *http://msdn.microsoft.com/library/ bb429645.aspx*.

The *Find* method has eleven optional parameters. You will use the first two parameters: *what* and *where*. You are not trying to find anything at first, so the *what* parameter will be null, and the *where* parameter will be *Atlanta, GA*. Because you want this to happen when the *Virtual Earth* control is loaded, you must add the following line to the *GetMap* function:

```
map.Find(null,'Atlanta, GA');
```

The final *GetMap* function will look like Listing 7-4.

LISTING 7-4 *GETMAP* FUNCTION WITH FIND METHOD

```
var map = null;
function GetMap()
{
```

```
    map = new VEMap('myMap');
    map.LoadMap(null, 10 ,'h' ,false);
    map.Find(null, 'Atlanta, GA');
}
```

To see the results, click **Run**. The browser window opens and shows the *Virtual Earth* control displaying a map of Atlanta, Georgia. (See Figure 7-5.)

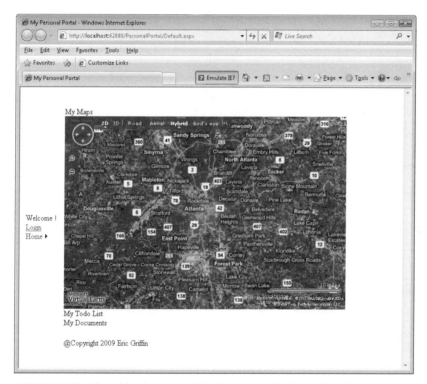

FIGURE 7-5 The *Virtual Earth* control displaying a map of Atlanta, Georgia.

Controlling the *Virtual Earth* Control with an HTML and a JavaScript Interface

You have taken one step closer to making the *Virtual Earth* control more useful to the user. However, as stated in the story in Chapter 4, Eric travels a lot as a consultant, so he might not be in Atlanta all the time. Also, he will definitely need to find things, such as a great pizza restaurant, when he is out of town.

You need an interface that enables Eric to find things quickly wherever he is. Before you create the interface, you need a function to help you. You already know that the *Find* method is a great way to specify *what* and *where*. That's how you specified the default location of the map as Atlanta. Let's wrap the *Find* method in a general function that can be called by controls on the browser to set *what* and *where*. Listing 7-5 shows a simple function that does just that.

LISTING 7-5 *FIND* FUNCTION

```
function Find(what,where)
{
    try
    {
        map.Find(what,where);
    }
    catch(e)
    {
        alert(e.message);
    }
}
```

This function should be added to the <script> tag in the PersonalPortal.master with the *GetMap* function. The function, also called *Find*, takes two parameters and passes them to the *map.Find* function. Remember that the map object was created in the *GetMap* function.

Now that you have defined the function, you need a way to interact with the user. The best approach is to allow the user to enter *what* and *where* by using an *HTML <input>* control. They should be above or below the control. Let's go with below the control. You can add them through the Visual Web Developer editor in Design mode, or you can type the controls manually in the *Content* display control.

> **Note** Because of the tight space defined in the Main.master markup, it might be difficult to drag the controls beneath the control in the editor.

You must also add some text labels so the user can know where to type. Listing 7-6 shows the markup for Default.aspx.

LISTING 7-6 DEFAULT.ASPX MARKUP WITH INPUT CONTROLS

```
<%@ Page Language="C#" AutoEventWireup="true" MasterPageFile="~/MasterPages/Main.master"
CodeFile="Default.aspx.cs" Inherits="_Default" %>
<asp:Content ID="Content1" ContentPlaceHolderID="MyMapContent" runat="server" >

    <div id='myMap' style="position:relative; width:600px; height:400px;" ></div>
        What:<input id="txtWhat" type="text" name="txtWhat" />
        Where:<input id="txtWhere" type="text" name="txtWhere" />
        <input id="find" type="button" value="Find" name="find"
onclick="Find(txtWhat.value,txtWhere.value);" />

</asp:Content>
```

Notice the *onclick* attribute. It is an event the HTML control will fire when the Find button is clicked: the JavaScript Find(txtWhat.value,txtWhere.value); statement is executed. It calls the function you created, with parameters being values from inputs for *what* and *where*, respectively. The controls in the Visual Web Developer editor look like Figure 7-6.

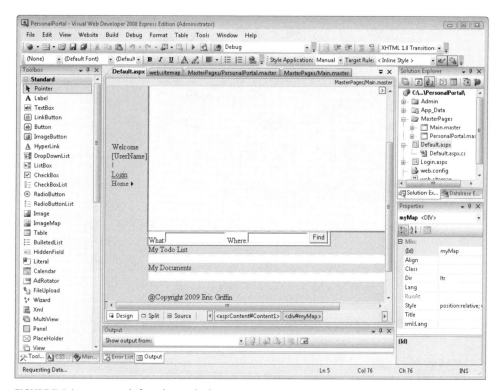

FIGURE 7-6 Input controls for *what* and *where*.

To see the results of your work, click **Run** from the standard toolbar. The browser opens to display the Virtual Earth map set to Atlanta. (See Figure 7-7.)

Enter **pizza** in the *What* input control and click **Find**. The results should look like Figure 7-8.

Pushpins appear on the *Virtual Earth* control, enabling you to hover over each pin to see the location and phone number. Let's say Eric doesn't live in the city but in the suburbs of Atlanta. Leave **pizza** in the *What* input control, type **Alpharetta** in the *Where* input control, and click **Find**. The *Virtual Earth* control moves to Alpharetta and displays the selection of pizza restaurants in the area. (See Figure 7-9.)

Eric could easily type the *what* and *where* to wherever he is located at the time. He could be in Miami, New York, or San Francisco.

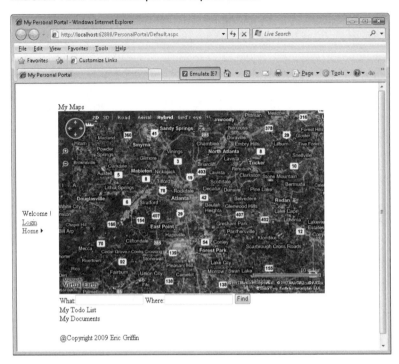

FIGURE 7-7 Input controls for *what* and *where* running in the browser.

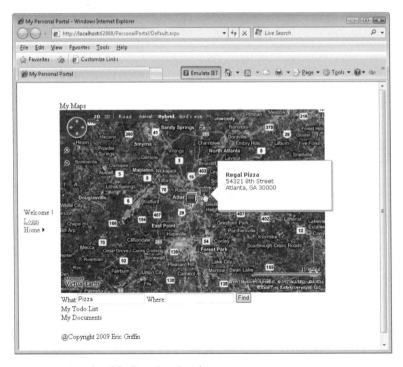

FIGURE 7-8 Results of finding pizza in Atlanta.

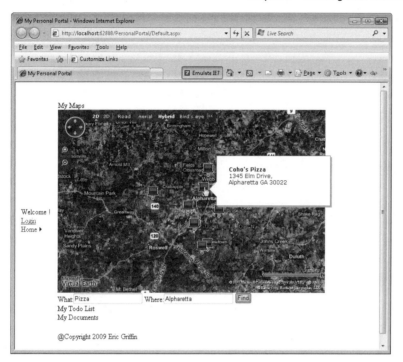

FIGURE 7-9 Results of finding pizza in Alpharetta, Georgia.

Debugging JavaScript in Visual Web Developer

You've added simple functionality to the personal portal by using JavaScript. However, as your JavaScript skills grow and you create more code in JavaScript, the opportunities for errors grow. Debugging is an important skill to help you find errors and test code. Visual Web Developer provides rich capabilities for debugging JavaScript on the client in browsers. The same techniques you use here can be used with C# code on the server. You will explore debugging in C# in later chapters.

Debugging with Visual Web Developer is capable only with Microsoft Internet Explorer. By default, the capability for debugging with Internet Explorer is disabled.

Enable debugging in Internet Explorer with Visual Web Developer

1. Select Internet Options from the Tools menu.

2. When the Internet Options dialog box appears, click the **Advanced** tab.

3. In the **Browsing** section, clear the **Disable script debugging (Internet Explorer)** check box. (See Figure 7-10.)

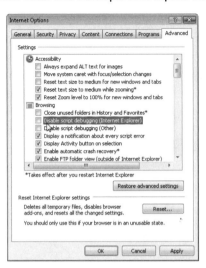

FIGURE 7-10 Internet Options dialog box.

4. Return to Visual Web Developer with the Personal Portal project open. Right-click the project and select **Start Options**. (See Figure 7-11.)

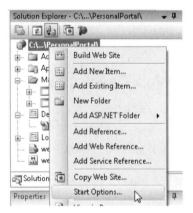

FIGURE 7-11 Virtual Earth Interactive SDK.

5. When the Start Options dialog box appears, clear the ASP.NET check box. (See Figure 7-12.)

Remember to select this check box when you want to debug server code.

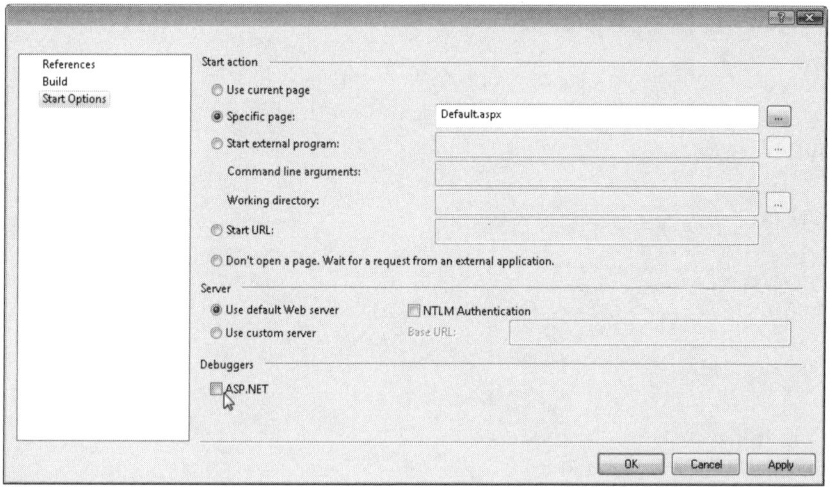

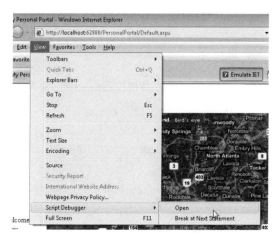

FIGURE 7-12 Start Options dialog box.

Now that you have enabled both Internet Explorer and Visual Web Developer to debug JavaScript, you can try it out.

Click **Run**. The personal portal opens as it has before, with the *Virtual Earth* control set to Atlanta. Internet Explorer requires that you enable debugging explicitly by selecting **Script Debugger** from the **View** menu and then selecting **Open**. (See Figure 7-13.)

FIGURE 7-13 Enabling Internet Explorer Script Debugger.

Setting a Breakpoint

Debugging enables you to step, line by line, through JavaScript code. You can start debugging in several ways. The Debug menu is the central focus during debugging, as shown in Figure 7-14.

FIGURE 7-14 The Debug menu.

Choose **Step Into** and begin debugging from the first line of JavaScript. This might seem like a logical thing to do, but remember that you have generated a lot of markup and code by Visual Web Developer and the server controls, so you typically start inside of that JavaScript. Needless to say, it can be confusing and overwhelming.

A better technique is to set breakpoints in your JavaScript. This way, you can focus on a particular area in your JavaScript. Breakpoints stop the execution of JavaScript, enabling you to inspect the current executing code and execute code line by line.

You can set a breakpoint by using Toggle Breakpoint or by pressing the F9 shortcut. Let's create a breakpoint by returning to Visual Web Developer while the personal portal is running in debug mode. Set the breakpoint on a line of code in PersonalPortal.master as follows.

Debug the personal portal

1. Open **PersonalPortal.master** in Source mode in Visual Web Developer while the personal portal is running in debug mode.

   Make sure you have followed the steps to enable debugging in Internet Explorer.

2. Set a breakpoint by clicking the gray column to the far left of the PersonalPortal.master Map.Find(what,where)JavaScript code. Alternatively, you can place the cursor on the line of JavaScript and select Toggle Breakpoint or the F9 shortcut.

   The line should highlight in red with a red dot showing in the far left gray column. (See Figure 7-15.)

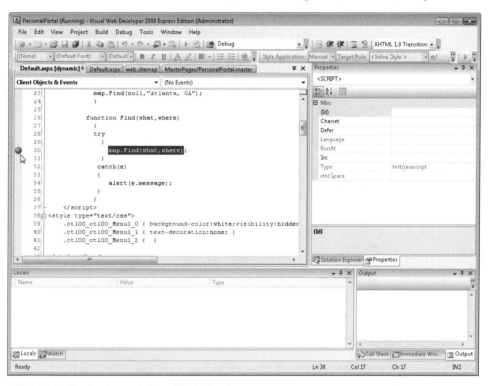

FIGURE 7-15 Breakpoint set in Visual Web Developer.

3. Now that the breakpoint is set, return to the browser and enter **Pizza** in the **What** input text box. Click **Find**.

Visual Web Developer will come to the front of the browser with the code where you set the highlighted breakpoint. (See Figure 7-16.)

```
23          map.Find(null,"Atlanta, GA");
24          }
25
26      function Find(what,where)
27          {
28          try
29              {
30                  map.Find(what,where);
31              }
32          catch(e)
33              {
34                  alert(e.message);
35              }
36          }
```

FIGURE 7-16 Execution stopped at the breakpoint.

4. Hover the mouse over the **what** variable to see the *"pizza"* value you entered in the *What* input text box. (See Figure 7-17.)

If you hover the mouse over the **where** variable, you will see that it is empty.

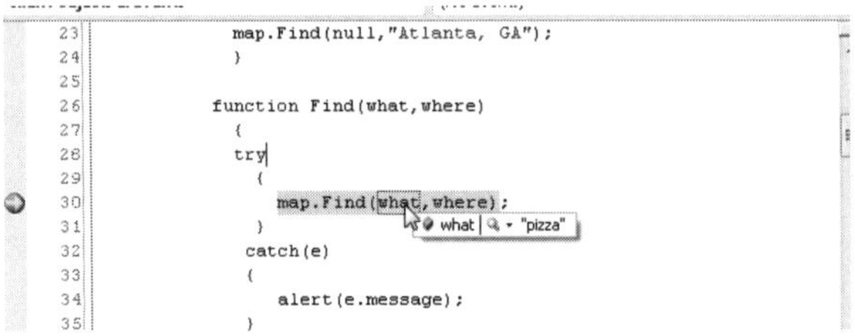

```
23         map.Find(null,"Atlanta, GA");
24       }
25
26       function Find(what,where)
27       {
28         try
29         {
30           map.Find(what, where);
31         }
32         catch(e)
33         {
34           alert(e.message);
35         }
```

FIGURE 7-17 Virtual Earth interactive SDK.

Also notice that a window called Locals has appeared at the bottom of the editor. A list of all the variables currently active is displayed with their values and types. (See Figure 7-18.)

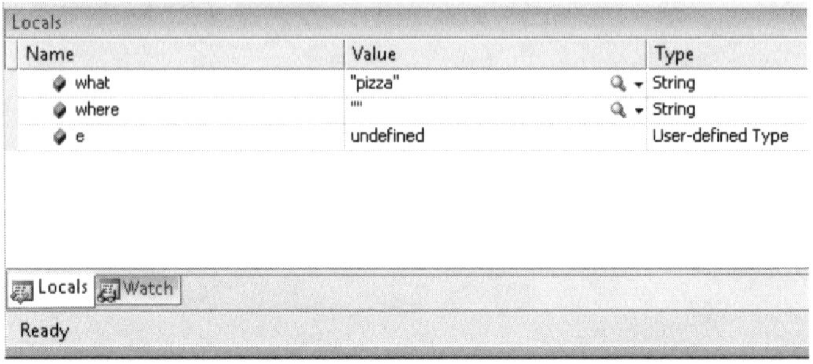

Name	Value		Type
what	"pizza"	Q ▾	String
where	""	Q ▾	String
e	undefined		User-defined Type

Locals Watch

Ready

FIGURE 7-18 Locals window.

The Locals window is a great way to inspect variables you might have set in a calculation instead of in a user interface element.

In the Locals window, you can also change the value of variables and then allow the code to continue execution to test different conditions. You entered "pizza" in the interface; now let's set the *where* variable while you are debugging.

5. Type **Alpharetta** in the Value column for the *where* variable in the Locals window. (See Figure 7-19.)

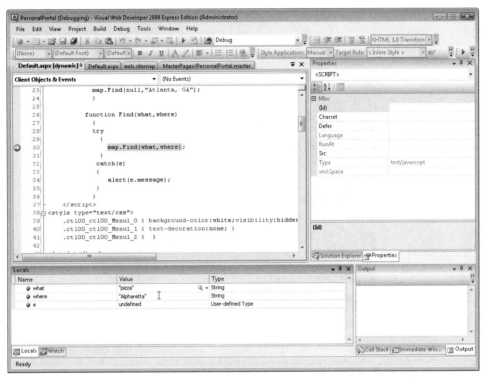

FIGURE 7-19 Setting the *where* value in the Locals window.

6. To see the results, click **Run** to continue running the personal portal with your variable change.

Figure 7-20 shows that the *"pizza" what* value is still in the input box where you originally typed it. The *where* text box is empty because you never typed a value in it. However, you know that the *where* variable was set while you were debugging, and the *Virtual Earth* control is set to the city of Alpharetta as if you typed it.

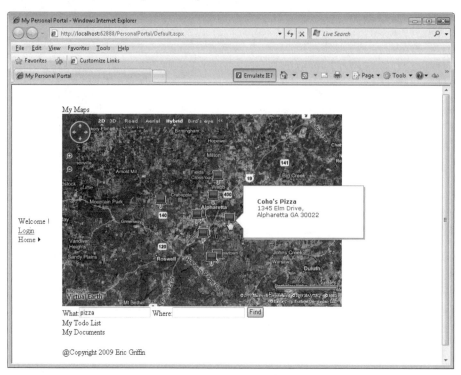

FIGURE 7-20 Results of setting the *where* value during debugging.

Explore debugging JavaScript further. Try typing in the *where* variable and then setting the *what* variable during debugging.

Summary

In this chapter, you learned how to integrate the *Virtual Earth* map control into the personal portal. You used JavaScript and HTML in the Visual Web Developer editor to do this. You also learned how to debug JavaScript. While debugging, you learned how to inspect JavaScript variable values and change them on the fly.

Chapter 8
Working with Databases

After completing this chapter, you will be able to

- Describe what a database is and how it is similar to a spreadsheet.

- Describe database data types.

- Describe what database tables are and how to define their structure.

- Create a database, using Database Explorer.

- Create a table, using Database Explorer.

- Create columns to represent rows of a table.

- Create rows in a table.

- Define Structured Query Language (SQL).

- Describe how to use the SELECT statements to retrieve data from tables.

- Describe how to use the WHERE clause to filter data retrieved from tables.

- Create SQL queries in SQL Query Designer.

All applications begin and end with data. Within applications, data is added, stored, and re-trieved. It is the value proposition of applications that helps you control your data. Databases are the central technology that helps applications organize, store, and retrieve data.

The personal portal is also an application that will help your user, Eric, control data that is important to him. From your story in Chapter 4, "Creating Your First Web Site," you know that Eric needs to manage his to-dos. A to-do can be regarded as a piece of data, so you need to create a database to organize, store, and retrieve to-do information. In this chapter, I will walk you through the process of creating the to-do database, using Visual Web Developer.

Brief Introduction to Databases

A database is a file that is structured to store data. A database can be as simple as a text file or as complicated as a commercial database package such as Microsoft SQL Server 2008.

 Note When you first installed Microsoft Visual Studio Web Developer in Chapter 2, "Working in Visual Web Developer 2008," you installed a free version of SQL Server called Visual SQL Server Express edition. You can read more about it at *http://microsoft.com/sql/editions/express /default.mspx*.

To give you an idea of how databases work, let's compare it to the first database technology: spreadsheets.

If you don't have access to a spreadsheet program such as Microsoft Excel, follow along with the screenshots to get an idea. Open Office Excel or some other spreadsheet program if you have it. (See Figure 8-1.)

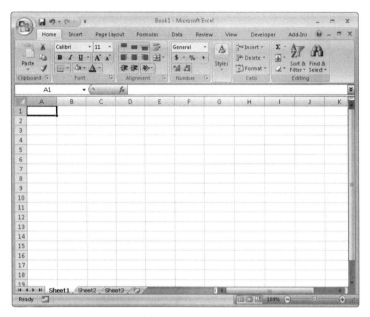

FIGURE 8-1 An empty spreadsheet.

A spreadsheet has cells, in which you can enter data, that are organized by columns hori-zontally and by rows vertically. If you think about to-dos and how they would need to be organized, each to-do needs a name to identify it, so make column A represent the name of the to-do. Keeping things simple, you just need to know whether the to-do has been done. Assign column B to indicate whether the to-do has be completed. To be consistent, the value in each column can be one of two value pairs: *Yes* or *No*, *Complete* or *Not Complete*, *Done* or *Not Done*, or *True* or *False*. *True* or *False* are called Boolean values, represented in C# by *0* and *1*. Let's use *True* or *False*.

Type some test values into the spreadsheet in the columns you indicated and add more than one row of data. The spreadsheet will look like Figure 8-2.

You now have two rows of data representing two to-dos. The to-do in row 1 has been com-pleted with a value in column B of *True*. The to-do in row 2 has not been completed. Also note that I have named the worksheet My To-dos to indicate that this worksheet is only for to-dos. Congratulations! You have created your first database.

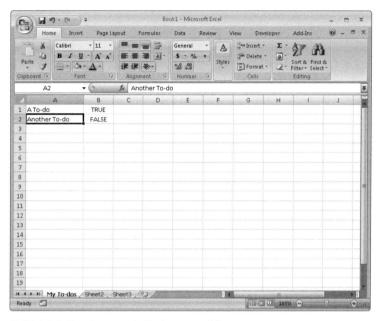

FIGURE 8-2 Creating a to-do list in a spreadsheet.

Database Software

You've just created a simple database by using a spreadsheet. Although many users use spreadsheets as databases, the best way to store and retrieve data is in database software.

Database software such as SQL Server 2008 is more complicated than spreadsheets, but the principle is the same. Figure 8-3 shows the basic structure of a database.

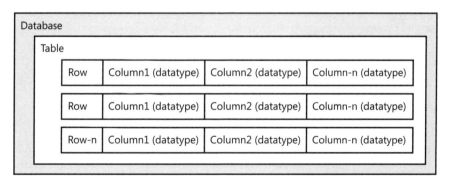

FIGURE 8-3 Live Search maps.

There are four concepts about databases you need to be familiar with: tables, rows, columns, and data types.

- **Tables**   Tables are like worksheets; they are defined to store a specific format of data in rows. A database can have one or more tables. The most complicated databases can have hundreds of tables.

- **Rows**   Rows are the contents of the table and are defined by columns. Like rows in spreadsheets, rows in databases can be uniquely identified and ordered.

- **Columns**   Columns are the contents of the row and are defined by data types. Similarly, cells in a spreadsheet can be formatted for a specific number to validate the values in the cell.

- **Data Types**   Data types define specific kinds of data. This helps you constrain the values for each column in a database table. You can use 25 data types in SQL Server:

EXACT NUMBERS

Type	From	To
bigint	-9,223,372,036,854,775,808	9,223,372,036,854,775,807
int	-2,147,483,648	2,147,483,647
smallint	-32,768	32,767
tinyint	0	255
bit	0	1
decimal	$-10\wedge38 +1$	$10\wedge38 -1$
numeric	$-10\wedge38 +1$	$10\wedge38 -1$
money	-922,337,203,685,477.5808	+922,337,203,685,477.5807
smallmoney	-214,748.3648	+214,748.3647

APPROXIMATE NUMBERS

Type	From	To
float	-1.79E + 308	1.79E + 308
real	-3.40E + 38	3.40E + 38

DATETIME AND SMALLDATETIME

Type	From	To
datetime (3.33 milliseconds accuracy)	Jan 1, 1753	Dec 31, 9999
smalldatetime (1 minute accuracy)	Jan 1, 1900	Jun 6, 2079

CHARACTER STRINGS

Type	Description
char	Fixed-length non-Unicode character data with a maximum length of 8,000 characters
varchar	Variable-length non-Unicode data with a maximum of 8,000 characters
varchar(max)	Variable-length non-Unicode data with a maximum length of 231 characters (SQL Server 2005 only)
text	Variable-length non-Unicode data with a maximum length of 2,147,483,647 characters

UNICODE CHARACTER STRINGS

Type	Description
nchar	Fixed-length Unicode data with a maximum length of 4,000 characters
nvarchar	Variable-length Unicode data with a maximum length of 4,000 characters
nvarchar(max)	Variable-length Unicode data with a maximum length of 230 characters (SQL Server 2005 only)
ntext	Variable-length Unicode data with a maximum length of 1,073,741,823 characters

BINARY STRINGS

Type	Description
binary	Fixed-length binary data with a maximum length of 8,000 bytes
varbinary	Variable-length binary data with a maximum length of 8,000 bytes
varbinary(max)	Variable-length binary data with a maximum length of 231 bytes (SQL Server 2005 only)
image	Variable-length binary data with a maximum length of 2,147,483,647 bytes

Table Relationships

Tables can also be related to more than one table by using keys. These keys can be defined and used to *join* two tables with related information. (See Figure 8-4.)

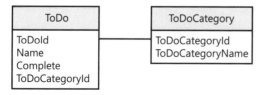

FIGURE 8-4 Table Relationships.

For example, you can relate the to-dos to a category of to-dos. A ToDo table is defined with a ToDoId as a unique identifier for each row in the table. A ToDoCategoryId links to a related table called ToDoCategory, which would store all the kinds of to-dos such as work, home, personal, and so on.

You can use keys defined in the ToDo (ToDoId) and ToDoCategory (ToDoCategoryId) tables to retrieve data in the ToDo table columns (Name, Complete) and the corresponding ToDoCategoryName column from the ToDoCategory table. The resulting join of both tables is called a *result set*.

Retrieving Rows by Using Structured Query Language

When you start talking about joins and result sets, you are talking about querying the tables in a database for rows of data. The querying is executed using a language called Structured Query Language, or SQL. As with JavaScript and C# statements, SQL statements have a syntax that can be used to create joins between tables and to retrieve data from databases.

Here are some examples of SQL statements.

SELECT Statements

The SELECT statement selects data from a table. The tabular result is stored in a result table called the result set. SQL statements are not case sensitive. SELECT is the same as select.

LISTING 8-1 Syntax of a SELECT Statement

```
SELECT <column_name(s)>
FROM <table_name>
```

To select all the rows (refer to Figure 8-4) with the columns named Name and Complete from the database table called ToDo, use a SELECT statement like this:

```
SELECT Name,Complete FROM ToDo
```

To select all the rows with the columns from the ToDo table, you can also use a SQL shortcut by typing a * symbol instead of column names, like this:

```
SELECT * FROM ToDo
```

WHERE Clauses

Sometimes you might need to filter the rows that are retrieved by SQL statements. You can select data conditionally from a table by using a WHERE clause.

LISTING 8-2 Syntax of a WHERE Clause

```
SELECT <column> FROM <table>
WHERE <column> <operator> <value>
```

With the WHERE clause, the following operators can be used:

Operator	Description
=	Equal
<>	Not equal
>	Greater than
<	Less than
>=	Greater than or equal
<=	Less than or equal
BETWEEN	Between an inclusive range
LIKE	Search for a pattern
IN	If you know the exact value you want to return for at least one of the columns

To select only the to-dos that have a complete value of *True*, you add a WHERE clause to the SELECT statement:

```
SELECT * FROM ToDo WHERE Complete = True
```

WHERE clauses can be even more complicated by adding additional operators and conditions by using the AND and OR keywords:

```
SELECT * FROM ToDo WHERE Complete = True AND ToDoCategoryId = 2
```

Learning More About Databases

I won't try to teach you everything about databases. Just the basics. Some professionals spend their entire careers trying to master databases. I can suggest a reference you can use to explore databases further: *Beginning SQL Server 2005 Express for Developers: From Novice to Professional*, by Robin Dewson (Apress, 2007)

Creating the ToDo Table in Visual Web Developer

You've examined the theories of databases, how they are structured with tables and how to store data using rows with columns of a type. You know that you want to track to-dos, so you will create a table to store the to-dos, called ToDo (see Figure 8-5), using Visual Web Developer.

FIGURE 8-5 The design of the ToDo table.

ToDoId

> Will represent the unique identifier for the rows in the table. It will be exactly like the spreadsheet. It will start with a value of 1 and increment by 1 for each new row.

Name

> Will represent what the to-do will be called by the users. They will be allowed to enter anything they want here.

Complete

> Will represent whether the to-do has been completed. This will be a Boolean value—true or false.

To create a database in Visual Web Developer

1. Start Visual Web Developer and open the **Personal Portal** project.

2. Right-click the **Personal Portal** project in **Solution Explorer** and select **Add New Item**.

3. When the **Add New Item** dialog box appears, select **SQL Server Database** from the list of templates. (See Figure 8-6.)

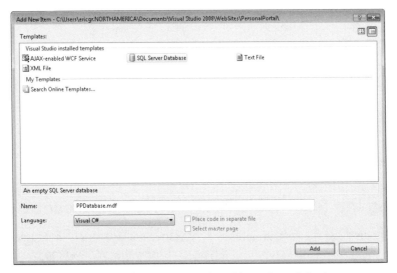

FIGURE 8-6 Adding a new database from the Add New Item dialog box.

4. Type **PPDatabase.mdf** in the **Name** field and click the **Add** button.

   A dialog box displays, asking you whether you want to place the new database in the App_Data folder.

5. Click **Yes**.

The dialog closes and returns you to Visual Web Developer Database Explorer. You will see the *ASPNETDB.MDF* above the PPDatabase.mdf you just created. (See Figure 8-7.)

FIGURE 8-7 Database Explorer shows the PPDatabase.mdf selected.

To create a table in Visual Web Developer

1. Double-click **PPDatabase.mdf** in **Database Explorer** to expand a list of folders representing the database objects.

2. Right-click the **Tables** folder. Select **Add New Table**. (See Figure 8-8.)

FIGURE 8-8 Add New Table.

A tab in the Visual Web Developer editor appears with the new table, called **Table1**.

This is your new table. Now you must customize it to have the structure of the ToDo table you have designed. (Refer to Figure 8-5.) To accomplish this customization, define the columns and their corresponding data types. From your design, you know you need to add three columns: ToDoId, Name, and Complete.

In the center of the editor is the Table Definition editor which contains three columns, called Column-Name, Data Type, and Allow Nulls, respectively. (See Figure 8-9.)

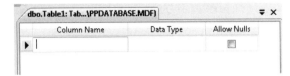

FIGURE 8-9 Table grid.

To define columns in a table in Visual Web Developer

1. Place the cursor in the first row of the **Table1** grid.

   Referring to Figure 8-9, this is where you add the name of the columns for the rows of the table.

2. Type **ToDoId** in the column name. Tab over or click in the **Data Type** column.

   A drop-down list of available SQL Server data types is displayed in the **Data Type** column.

3. Select the **int** data type.

   Notice that the **Allow Nulls** check box is automatically selected. See Figure 8-10.

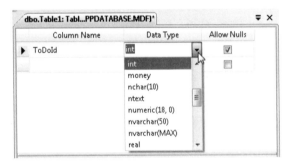

FIGURE 8-10 Adding the ToDoId column.

At bottom center of the editor is the **Column Properties** window. You can view or edit the properties of columns here also. (See Figure 8-11.)

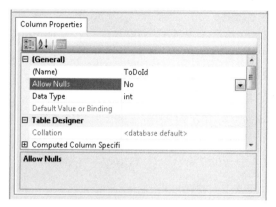

FIGURE 8-11 Column Properties.

The ToDoId column will uniquely identify the rows of data like the row numbers in a spreadsheet. In the spreadsheet example, the rows are numbered from 1 to 1.1 million rows (in Excel 2007). Databases duplicate this automatic numbering by specifying that the field is an identity field. Identity fields can be specified in the Column Properties window by scrolling down to the **Identity Specification** section.

4. Expand the **Identity Specification** section to see three property values: (*Is Identity*), *Identity Increment*, and *Identity Seed*.

5. While the **ToDoId** field is selected, choose **Yes** from the **(Is Identity)** property. (See Figure 8-12.)

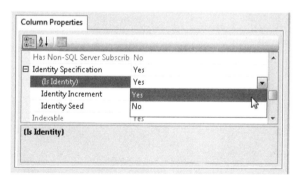

FIGURE 8-12 Setting the Identity property of the ToDoId field.

You can also change the default **Identity Increment** of 1 and the default **Identity Seed** of 1. This allows you to set up any complex incremental system you want. Also notice that the **Allow Nulls** check box is now cleared because there must be a generated value in the field.

6. Return to the **Table1** grid and create a new column called **Name**.

7. Select a data type of **varchar(50).**

The **Allow Nulls** field is selected automatically again.

8. You know that the name of a to-do can be longer than 50 characters, so add more room by returning to the **Column Properties** window, with the **Name** column selected, and type **100** in the length property.

This changes the data type from varchar(50) to varchar(100).

The last column will represent whether the to-do has been completed. In the spreadsheet, you represented this with a *TRUE* or *FALSE* value. A bit data type represents 0 and 1, so it would be the ideal choice for a Boolean value.

9. Return to the table grid and create a new column called **Complete**.

10. Select **bit** from the Data Type drop-down list.

The **Allow Nulls** check box is selected automatically again. The table definition should look like Figure 8-13.

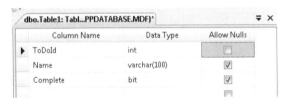

FIGURE 8-13 The ToDo table definition.

The table is still named Table1.

To save the table definition and name it ToDo

1. Open the **Properties** window.

2. Type **ToDo** in the **Name** property of the table. (See Figure 8-14.)

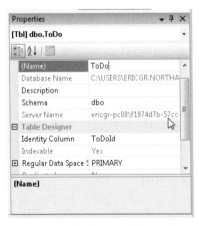

FIGURE 8-14 Naming the ToDo table.

3. Right-click the table definition editor and select **Save ToDo**. (See Figure 8-15.)

FIGURE 8-15 Saving the To-do table.

After the table is saved, it will display in the **Tables** folder in Database Explorer.

4. Double-click the **ToDo** table.

The table will expand to show the columns you defined in the **Table Definition Editor**. (See Figure 8-16.)

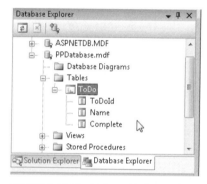

FIGURE 8-16 The ToDo table in Database Explorer.

5. Click each column.

You can see the properties displayed in the **Properties** window. You can make changes if you need to here. If you want to edit the **ToDo** table in the **Table Definition Editor** again, you can double-click it or right-click it and select **Open Table**.

Creating Rows in the ToDo Table

You have created the ToDo table and the columns that will represent rows of individual to-dos. Now you can test your table by adding rows, using Visual Web Developer Database Explorer.

To add rows to the ToDo table

1. Right-click the **ToDo** table in **Database Explorer** and select **Show Table Data**. (See Figure 8-17.)

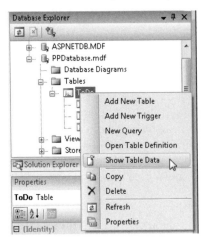

FIGURE 8-17 Selecting Show Table Data for the ToDo table.

A grid with the ToDo table columns, ToDoId, Name, and Complete, displays at the top horizontally. The first row has an asterisk in the far left, unmarked column. (See Figure 8-18.)

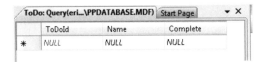

FIGURE 8-18 ToDo table with no rows of data.

2. Click in the grid in the Name column and type **A To do**.

   The *ToDoId* field is not editable.

3. Press the **Tab** key to advance to the Compete column.

   You will see a red exclamation point. It is a warning that the cell data has changed but has not been committed to the database. (See Figure 8-19.)

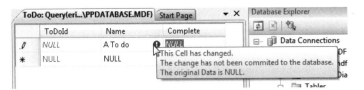

FIGURE 8-19 ToDo table with uncommitted data.

4. This to-do will be not completed, so type **False** in the **Complete** field and press **Enter**.

   Notice that when you finished typing in the *Complete* field, the *ToDoId* field was filled in with a value of *1* automatically. (See Figure 8-20.)

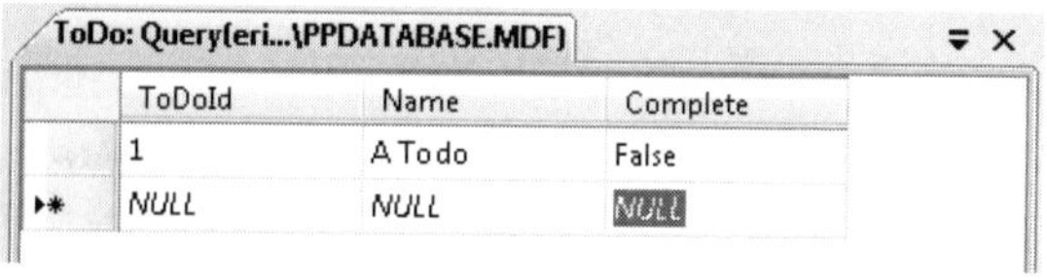

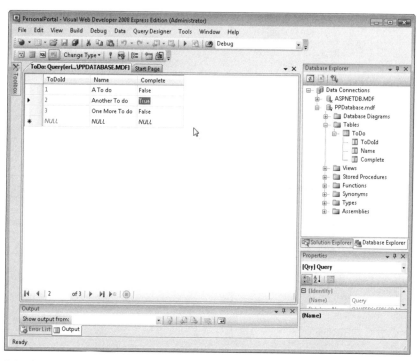

FIGURE 8-20 One row of data in the ToDo table.

5. Move to the next row indicated by an arrow and an asterisk and type **Another To do** in the Name column and **True** in the Complete column.

6. Add another row with **One More To do** in the Name and **False** in the Complete column.

Your table should be filled with three rows. (See Figure 8-21.)

FIGURE 8-21 ToDo table with three rows.

Querying Tables by Using Database Explorer

Now that you have data in your table, you can retrieve it. You do this by using SQL. Fortunately, Visual Web Developer has a Query editor in Database Explorer to help you build SQL.

To create a new SQL query, using Database Explorer

1. Return to Database Explorer, right-click the **ToDo** table, and select **New Query**. (See Figure 8-22.)

FIGURE 8-22 The New Query menu item.

The Add Table dialog box will appear, prompting you to choose which tables you want to use in the query. (See Figure 8-23.)

2. Because you will use only the ToDo table, select the **ToDo** table on the Tables tab in the dialog box and click the **Add button**.

3. Click **Close** to close the dialog box and return to Visual Web Developer.

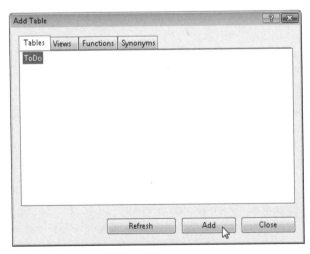

FIGURE 8-23 The Add Table dialog box.

The Query designer uses several areas when you are creating your query. (See Figure 8-24.)

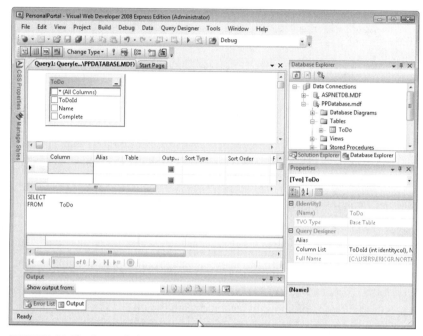

FIGURE 8-24 The Query designer.

The Query Designer Toolbar

A new toolbar for the Query designer has been added below the standard toolbar. From left to right and top to bottom, refer to Figure 8-25.

FIGURE 8-25 The Query designer.

Show Diagram Pane

Toggles the display of the Diagram pane at the top section of the editor.

Show Criteria Pane

Toggles the display of the Column selection criteria.

Show SQL Pane

Toggles the display of the text of the SQL query.

Show Results Pane

Toggles the display of the grid that displays the results of queries.

Change Type

Shows the types of queries.

The Query designer can create six types of queries. You will use the Select query type. The other types are Insert Results, Insert Values, Update, Delete, and Make Table.

Execute SQL

Runs the SQL text in the SQL pane.

Verify SQL Syntax

Validates the SQL text in the SQL pane.

The top section contains all the tables you have added, using the Add Table dialog box, and all the tables you will use in the query. The middle section contains the columns that will be used, and the bottom section shows you the resulting SQL.

Without any columns selected, the SQL looks like this:

```
SELECT
FROM ToDo
```

It looks like a start of SQL you can use, but a couple of things are missing. To demonstrate this, click the **Execute SQL** button on the Query designer toolbar. An error dialog box appears, stating that no columns are selected. (See Figure 8-26.)

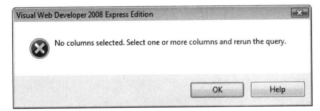

FIGURE 8-26 Error dialog box, stating that columns need to be selected.

Click **OK** to close the dialog box.

To create a SELECT SQL statement in the Query designer

Let's start building the query from the **Diagram** pane.

1. Choose the **ToDoId**, **Name**, and **Complete** fields by selecting their respective check boxes. (See Figure 8-27.)

    Notice in Figure 8-27 that the SQL in the SQL pane has changed to:

    ```
    SELECT ToDoId,Name,Complete
    FROM ToDo
    ```

    Also notice that the Criteria pane has an Output column in which each column is selected. As you can guess, the Output column can be used to include or exclude columns from a table.

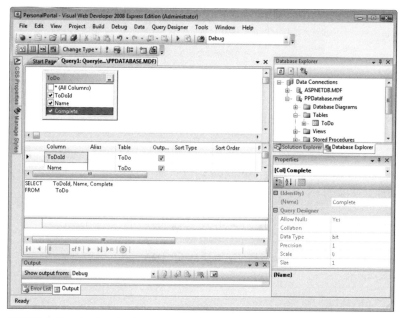

FIGURE 8-27 Selecting the fields in the ToDo table.

2. Execute the query by clicking the **Execute SQL** button. The results appear in the Results pane below the SQL pane. (See Figure 8-28.)

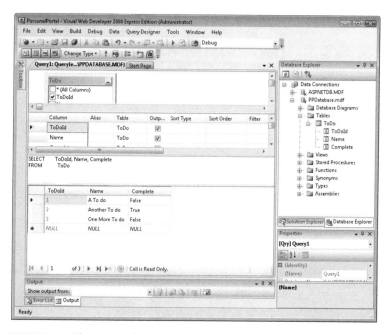

FIGURE 8-28 The results of the SELECT SQL statement.

ToDoId displays all the table rows in order, from 1 to 3, similar to the spreadsheet. Note that you could have used the * to choose all the fields. The SQL would be:

```
SELECT *
FROM ToDo
```

 Note If you do type the * in the SQL pane, the Query designer will automatically add all the columns of the table.

But what if you wanted to select only the to-do that has been completed? You would have to add a WHERE clause to the SQL.

To add a WHERE clause to the SQL select statement

1. Type the **WHERE** clause directly in the SQL pane until your code looks like the following:

```
SELECT ToDoId,Name,Complete
FROM ToDo
WHERE Complete ='True'
```

The Filter column of the *Complete* field is automatically updated, and the SQL in the SQL pane is formatted. (See Figure 8-29.)

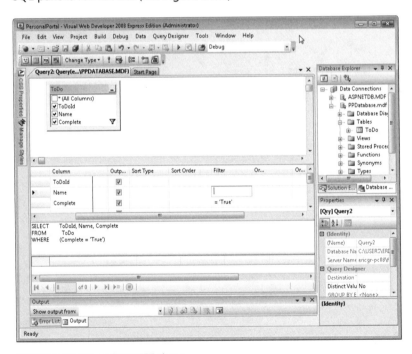

FIGURE 8-29 SQL with WHERE clause.

Before you execute the SQL query, let's verify that it is valid.

2. Click the **Verify SQL Syntax** button to the right of the Execute SQL button.

    The dialog box in Figure 8-30 displays.

FIGURE 8-30 SQL Validation dialog box.

3. Click **OK** to close the dialog box and click the **Execute SQL** button to run the SQL.

    The results show in the **Results** pane. (See Figure 8-31.)

	ToDoId	Name	Complete
▶	2	Another Todo	True
✱	NULL	NULL	NULL

|◀ ◀ | 1   of 1 | ▶ ▶| ▶✱ | ⬤ | Cell is Read Only.

FIGURE 8-31 Results from the WHERE clause.

You've learned the very basics of creating databases, tables, and queries. Use some of the references mentioned earlier in this chapter to learn more about creating SQL queries and explore what you have learned about using the Query designer.

Summary

In this chapter, you learned how to create a database. You learned that a database consists of one or more tables, which are structured with columns of specific types to contain the values stored within the database. These columns are used to make rows of values for the user or application to fill in. Tables can be queried for their rows, using a technology called Structured Query Language (SQL). SQL statements can retrieve and filter data in tables. The ToDo table you created in this chapter will be used in the next chapter when you design and build an interface to it in the personal portal.

Chapter 9
Building Data-Driven User Interfaces

After completing this chapter, you will be able to

- Create a data set.

- Configure an existing table adapter.

- Create a new table adapter.

- Create a parameterized SQL SELECT query.

- Create a grid view to display rows of data.

- Create a parameterized SQL UPDATE query.

- Configure a grid view to edit rows of data.

- Create a data source.

- Create a *DetailsView* data control to add new rows of data.

In the preceding chapter, you learned about databases and Structured Query Language (SQL). In this chapter, you create an interface in the personal portal to manage the to-dos in the *ToDo* database you created. Figure 9-1 shows the *ToDo* database in Visual Web Developer Data Explorer.

Visual Web Developer has data controls to help you build data-driven interfaces quickly in .NET with little code. The technology the data controls use in .NET is called Active Data Objects (ADO). ADO.NET has Microsoft Visual C# objects that enable you to connect and query databases.

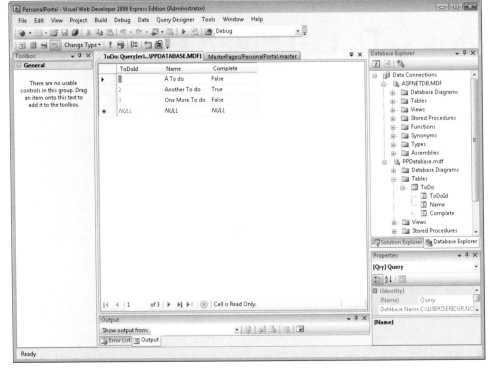

FIGURE 9-1 *ToDo* database.

Data Sets

A key ADO.NET technology used by the Visual Web Developer data controls to manage the connection and query a database is the data set. Data sets are an in-memory cache of data retrieved from a data source and are consumed by the data controls, so before you can create an interface, you must create a data set.

To create a data set for the *ToDo* database

1. Start Visual Web Developer and open the **Personal Portal** project.

2. Right-click the Personal Portal project and select **Add New Item**.

3. When the Add New Item dialog box appears, select **DataSet** from the Templates list.

4. Type **ToDoDataSet.xsd** in the *Name* field. (See Figure 9-2.)

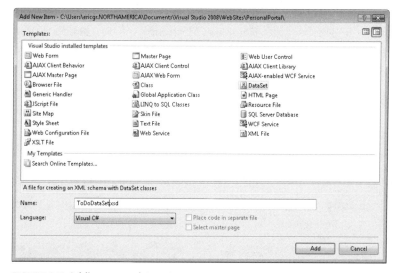

FIGURE 9-2 Adding a new data set.

5. Click **Add**.

   A dialog box will appear that will ask whether you want to create a folder called App_ Code in the Personal Portal project. (See Figure 9-3.) This is the recommended folder for data sets and C# objects that are not related to .aspx pages.

FIGURE 9-3 Create App_Code folder dialog box.

6. Click **Yes** to create **ToDoDataSet.xsd** and place it in the newly created **App_Code** folder. (See Figure 9-4.)

FIGURE 9-4 ToDoDataSet.xsd.

Now that you have created the dataset, configure it to connect to the ToDo table you created in Chapter 8, "Working with Databases." Currently, the data set displays a message on the design surface that indicates that database items can be dragged onto the surface to configure the data set. Let's do just that.

To configure a data set to a table

1. Open **PPDatabase.mdf** in **Database Explorer**.

   Remember, you can access it by using the Database Explorer tab.

2. Click **PPDatabase.mdf** to show the Tables folder and then the **ToDo** table.

3. Drag the **ToDo** table onto the data set design surface to configure the data set to the ToDo table. (See Figure 9-5.)

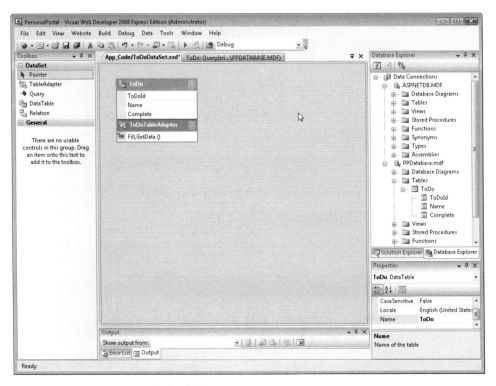

FIGURE 9-5 The ToDo data set in the designer.

On the design surface, you can see that the data set shows the format of the ToDo table, as shown in Figure 9-6. It shows all the columns that are defined in it. What you have defined is called a data table. Data sets can contain one or more data tables, like a database can contain tables. Because data sets mirror a database, they can be used like a virtual database. This enables the application that uses the data set to be disconnected and offline from the database.

FIGURE 9-6 The ToDo data set.

Table Adapters

In Figure 9-6, you see another icon, called ToDo TableAdapter. Table adapters are another ADO.NET technology. Whereas data tables define the table structure and store rows of data, table adapters are how you can add, update, and delete data stored in a data table.

If you examine the ToDo TableAdapter section of the ToDo data table in the ToDoDataSet.xsd design surface, you see that a *Fill* method has already been created.

To configure an existing *TableAdapter* method

1. Right-click the **Fill** method on the method in **ToDoTableAdapter**.

2. Select **Configure**. (See Figure 9-7.)

FIGURE 9-7 Configuring a *Fill* method.

The TableAdapter Configuration Wizard opens. (See Figure 9-8.) You can see the SQL used to query the ToDo table in PPDatabase.mdf. You can edit the SQL directly in the text box or use Query Builder by clicking **Query Builder**.

3. You will not make any modifications to the method, so click **Cancel**.

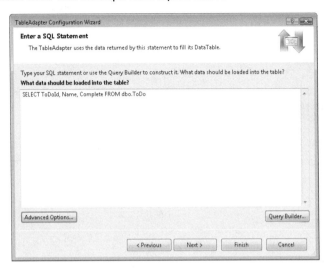

FIGURE 9-8 TableAdapter Configuration Wizard.

The TableAdapter *Fill* method, by examining the SQL, can retrieve data and add rows to the ToDo data table. However, as it exists now, it would not meet the requirements for an interface for Eric, your user. He will want to see what to-dos are completed. The SQL in the *Fill* method returns the ToDoId, Name, and Complete columns from the ToDo table but doesn't enable you to filter the data based on the Complete column. What is missing is a WHERE clause and a way for your interface to send a dynamic parameter to specify whether you want to return completed to-dos.

You can modify the existing method, but let's create a new one from scratch.

To create a *TableAdapter* method

1. Right-click the **ToDo TableAdapter** section in the ToDoDataSet.xsd design surface.

2. Select the **Add Query** menu item from the menu.

    The TableAdapter Query Configuration Wizard dialog box displays. It gives you three options: to use SQL, to create a new table adapter method, or to use an existing stored procedure.

> **Note** Stored procedures are database platform–embedded SQL functions. Stored procedures are advanced functionality and are beyond the scope of this book. Please use the books mentioned in Chapter 8 to explore stored procedures.

3. You won't be using stored procedures, so leave the default Use SQL Statements. (See Figure 9-9.)

4. Click **Next**.

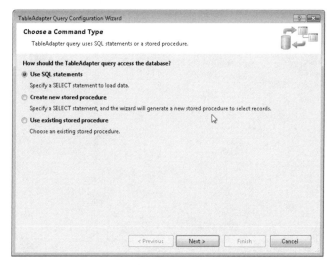

FIGURE 9-9 Leaving the default Use SQL Statements.

The next page in the wizard gives you five choices, as shown in Figure 9-10. They are the basic types of SQL statements you can create: SELECT, UPDATE, DELETE, and INSERT.

5. You will create a SELECT statement, so leave the default SELECT, which returns rows.

6. Click **Next**.

FIGURE 9-10 Choose A Query Type page.

The next page enables you to modify the SELECT statement it supplies by default. (See Figure 9-11.)

7. Click **Query Builder**.

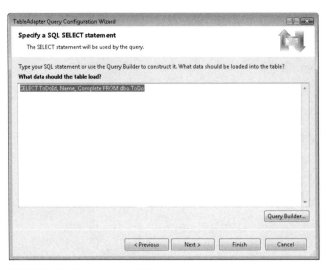

FIGURE 9-11 TableAdapter SQL.

The Query Builder dialog box appears with the ToDo table added and the ToDoId, Name, and Complete columns selected, as shown in Figure 9-12.

8. In the SQL pane, at the end of the SQL statement, type **WHERE Complete = @ IsComplete**.

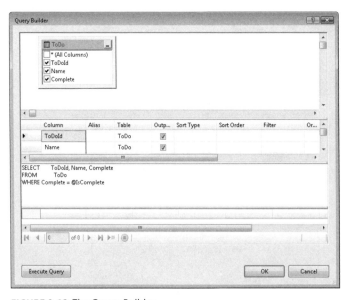

FIGURE 9-12 The Query Builder.

You should be familiar with the WHERE clause from Chapter 8. However, the filter is set to @IsComplete. Using the @ symbol is a way to create a SQL parameter for a query. This allows a parameter to be set dynamically. In this case, the parameter is named *IsComplete*.

9. To see how this works, click **Execute Query**.

   The Query Parameters dialog box displays. (See Figure 9-13.)

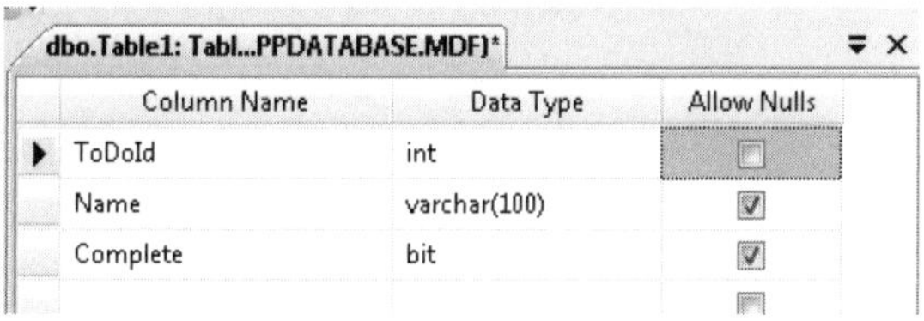

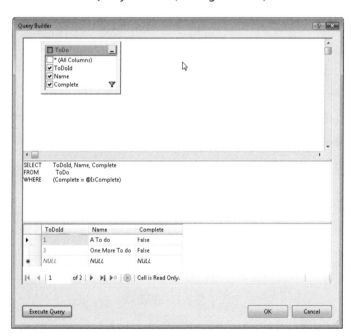

FIGURE 9-13 Query Parameters dialog box.

10. Type **False** in the Value column for the named parameter **@IsComplete**.

11. Click **OK**.

   The Query Parameters dialog box closes, and the results of the query display at the bottom of the Query Builder. (See Figure 9-14.)

FIGURE 9-14 The query results.

12. Now that you have tested your query, click **OK** to close the Query Builder.

   The TableAdapter Query Configuration Wizard displays the updated SQL. (See Figure 9-15.)

13. Click **Next**.

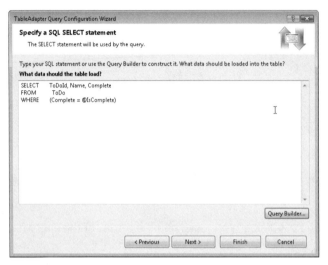

FIGURE 9-15 Updated SQL

The next wizard step asks which methods you want to add to the table adapter. (See Figure 9-16.)

14. Clear the **Fill a DataTable** check box and select **Return a DataTable**.

   The returned data table will be consumed by a user interface data control.

15. Type **GetToDoByStatus** in the *Method name* field to represent what the query is doing.

16. Click **Next**.

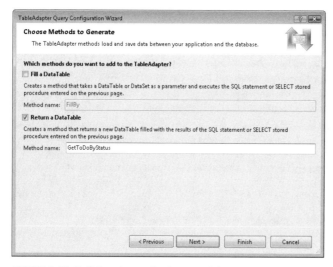

FIGURE 9-16 Defining the method name of the query.

The next page is the last. (See Figure 9-17.) It indicates that the TableAdapter query has been successfully configured.

17. Click **Finish**.

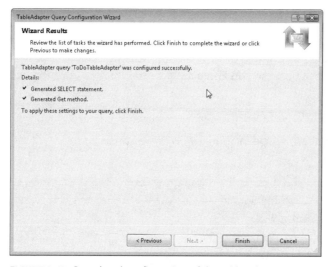

FIGURE 9-17 Completed configuration of the table adapter.

Creating a User Interface with Data Controls

The data controls in Visual Web Developer enable you to use the data set you defined to query the *ToDo* database. Now you must decide where to place it. If you recall the Main.master page you created in Chapter 5, "Using Master Pages," you know that you created content placeholders for the map called MyMapContent, documents called MyDocumentContent, and to-dos called MyTodoContent.

Now, add a Content control on the Default.aspx page. Type the *Content* control into the Default.aspx markup until it looks exactly like Listing 9-1.

LISTING 9-1 Adding MyTodoContent

```
<%@ Page Language="C#" AutoEventWireup="true" MasterPageFile="~/MasterPages/Main.master"
CodeFile="Default.aspx.cs" Inherits="_Default" %>

<asp:Content ID="Content1" ContentPlaceHolderID="MyMapContent" runat="server" >

    <div id='myMap' style="position:relative; width:600px; height:400px;" ></div>
        What:<input id="txtWhat" type="text" name="txtWhat" />
        Where:<input id="txtWhere" type="text" name="txtWhere" />
        <input id="find" type="button" value="Find" name="find" onclick="Find(txtWhat.
value,txtWhere.value);" />

</asp:Content>

<asp:Content ID="myTodos" ContentPlaceHolderID="MyTodoContent" runat="server">


</asp:Content>
```

You have defined the *Content* control that will hold the interface for the *ToDo* database. The first thing you must do is allow your user, Eric, to select completed or not completed to-dos. The best way to handle this is with a drop-down list. Note that this list doesn't have to be connected to a database because you know it will contain static values that won't change.

To create a *DropDownList* control

1. Open the Default.aspx page in Source view. Type **Status**: in the *MyTodoContent Content* control.

2. Open the Toolbox and expand the Standard section. Drag the *DropDownList* control from the Toolbox onto the Source view below the Status: text you typed. The code should look like Listing 9-2.

LISTING 9-2 DropDownList Added

```
<asp:Content ID="myTodos" ContentPlaceHolderID="MyTodoContent" runat="server">
Status:
    <asp:DropDownList ID="DropDownList1" runat="server">
    </asp:DropDownList>
</asp:Content>
```

3. Switch to **Design** view. Select **DropDownList** as shown Figure 9-18.

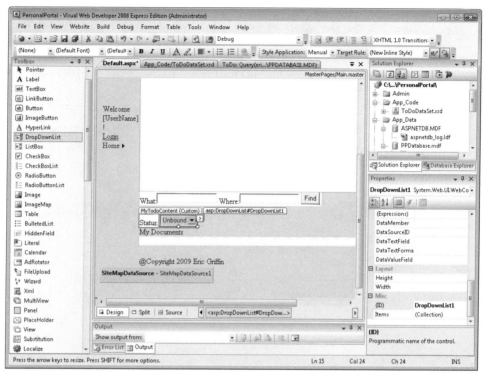

FIGURE 9-18 Selected DropDownList in the designer.

4. Click the configuration arrow and select **Enable AutoPostBack**. (See Figure 9-19.)

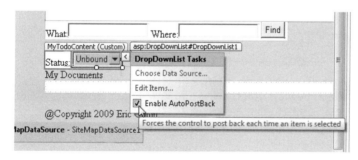

FIGURE 9-19 Configuring DropDownList.

5. Select **Edit Items** to display **List Item Collection Editor**.

6. Click **Add** twice to add two items to the Members pane.

7. Select the first item and type **Not Done** in the *Text* field of the properties pane.

8. Set Selected to **True**. Set Value to **False**.

> **Note** The *Text* and *Value* fields serve different purposes. The *Text* field is what the user will see in the drop-down list as an item. If that item is selected, the content of the *Value* field can be used to represent value meaningful to the application, such as a number or a Boolean value. In this case, you use the *Value* field to send that value to the *@IsCompleted SQL* parameter you created in the table adapter.

9. Select the second item and type **Done** in the *Text* field of the properties pane.

10. Set Selected to **False**. Set Value to **True**. (See Figure 9-20.)

11. Click **OK**.

FIGURE 9-20 List Item Collection Editor

If you return to the Source view, you can see that Visual Web Developer has added the properties in markup. (See Listing 9-3.)

LISTING 9-3 ADDING DROPDOWNLIST

```
<asp:Content ID="myTodos" ContentPlaceHolderID="MyTodoContent" runat="server">
Status:
    <asp:DropDownList ID="DropDownList1" runat="server" AutoPostBack="True">
        <asp:ListItem Selected="True" Value="False">Not Done</asp:ListItem>
        <asp:ListItem Value="True">Done</asp:ListItem>
    </asp:DropDownList>
</asp:Content>
```

The next part of the user interface to add is the list of to-dos. You can use a *GridView* control to accomplish this. Before you add the grid view, place a title above it. Within <div> tags, place the title, **To-do List**.

Next, drag a *GridView* control from the Data section of the Toolbox below the enclosing <div> tag. Your markup should look like Listing 9-4.

LISTING 9-4 Tile and GridView Control for To-dos

```
<asp:Content ID="myTodos" ContentPlaceHolderID="MyTodoContent" runat="server">
Status:
    <asp:DropDownList ID="DropDownList1" runat="server" AutoPostBack="True">
        <asp:ListItem Selected="True" Value="False">Not Done</asp:ListItem>
        <asp:ListItem Value="True">Done</asp:ListItem>
    </asp:DropDownList>
    <div>
     To-do List
    </div>
    <asp:GridView ID="GridView1" runat="server">
    </asp:GridView>

</asp:Content>
```

Now you can configure the *GridView* control to display data from the ToDo table, using the ToDo data set and the filter values from the status DropDownList.

To configure the *GridView* control

1. Switch to **Design** view if you are in Source view. (See Figure 9-21.)

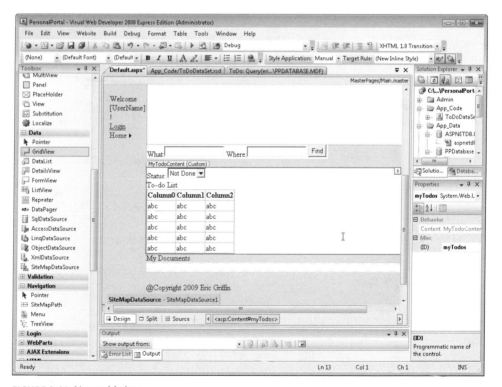

FIGURE 9-21 New grid view.

2. Select the **GridView** control in the *MyTodoContent* control. Select <**New data source**> from the Choose Data Source drop-down list. (See Figure 9-22.)

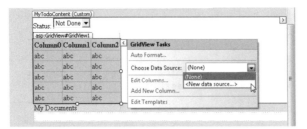

FIGURE 9-22 Selecting from Choose Data Source.

The Data Source Configuration Wizard displays. (See Figure 9-23.)

3. Select **Object** from the options for the source of data. Click **OK**.

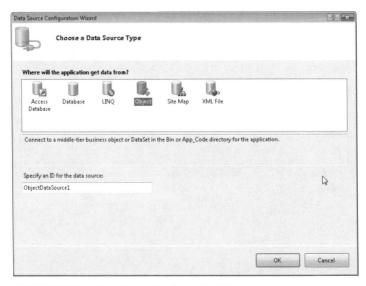

FIGURE 9-23 The Data Source Configuration Wizard.

The next page in the wizard displays.

4. Select **ToDoDataSetTableAdapters.ToDoTableAdapter** from the drop-down menu. (See Figure 9-24.)

5. Click **Next**.

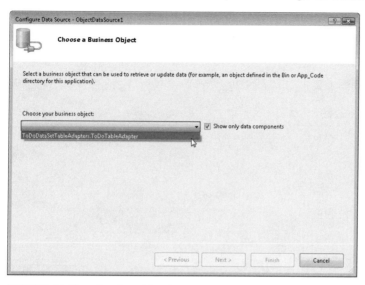

FIGURE 9-24 Choosing the table adapter.

On the next page, you set up the parameter you created in ToDoTableAdapter. (See Figure 9-25.)

6. Select **Control** from the Parameter Source drop-down menu. Select **DropDownList1** from the ControlID drop-down menu. Click **Finish**.

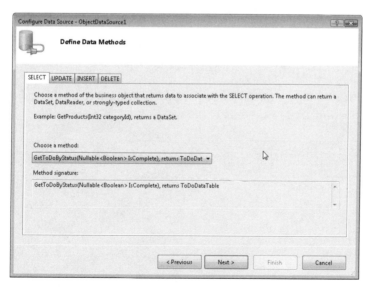

FIGURE 9-25 The Configure Data Source page.

The *GridView* control in Design view displays the fields in the ToDo table. Notice that the data source created by the wizard, ObjectDataSource1, has a visual representation below the grid view. (See Figure 9-26.)

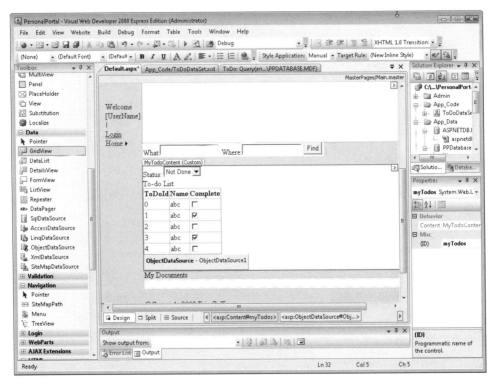

FIGURE 9-26 *GridView* and ObjectDataSource in the designer.

Click the **GridView** configuration arrow, select **Enable Paging** to display more to-dos, and select **Enable Sorting**. (See Figure 9-27.)

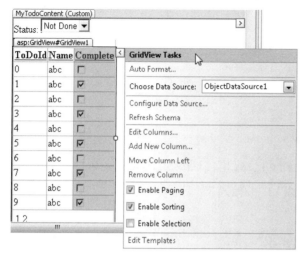

FIGURE 9-27 *GridView* configuration menu.

Switching to Source view, you can see the markup generated by the configuration options. (See Listing 9-5.)

LISTING 9-5 *GRIDVIEW* AND *DROPDOWNLIST*

```
<asp:Content ID="myTodos" ContentPlaceHolderID="MyTodoContent" runat="server">
Status:
    <asp:DropDownList ID="DropDownList1" runat="server" AutoPostBack="True">
        <asp:ListItem Selected="True" Value="False">Not Done</asp:ListItem>
        <asp:ListItem Value="True">Done</asp:ListItem>
    </asp:DropDownList>
    <div>
     To-do List
    </div>
    <asp:GridView ID="GridView1" runat="server" AllowPaging="True"
        AllowSorting="True" AutoGenerateColumns="False"
        DataSourceID="ObjectDataSource1">
        <Columns>
            <asp:BoundField DataField="ToDoId" HeaderText="ToDoId" InsertVisible="False"
                ReadOnly="True" SortExpression="ToDoId" />
            <asp:BoundField DataField="Name" HeaderText="Name" SortExpression="Name" />
            <asp:CheckBoxField DataField="Complete" HeaderText="Complete"
                SortExpression="Complete" />
        </Columns>
    </asp:GridView>

    <asp:ObjectDataSource ID="ObjectDataSource1" runat="server"
        InsertMethod="Insert" OldValuesParameterFormatString="original_{0}"
        SelectMethod="GetToDoByStatus"
        TypeName="ToDoDataSetTableAdapters.ToDoTableAdapter">
        <SelectParameters>
            <asp:ControlParameter ControlID="DropDownList1" Name="IsComplete"
                PropertyName="SelectedValue" Type="Boolean" />
        </SelectParameters>
        <InsertParameters>
```

```
        <asp:Parameter Name="Name" Type="String" />
        <asp:Parameter Name="Complete" Type="Boolean" />
    </InsertParameters>
  </asp:ObjectDataSource>

</asp:Content>
```

Now that you have the *GridView* and *DropDownList* controls to filter the complete or not-completed to-dos, you're ready to see it in action.

Click **Run**. After you log in, you should see the Microsoft Virtual Earth map and, below it, the Status drop-down list and the grid displaying the Not Done (the default value of *False*) to-dos. (See Figure 9-28.)

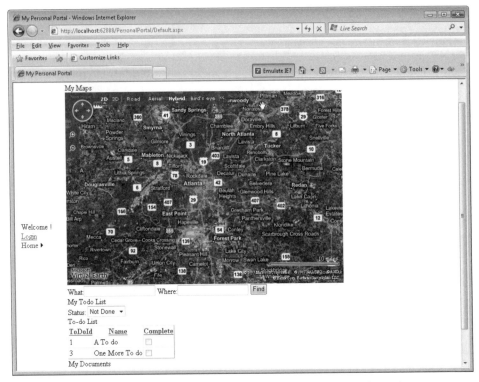

FIGURE 9-28 Using the Status drop-down list and the grid view in the personal portal.

Try selecting **Done** from the Status drop-down list and see the page refresh with the to-do that is complete, as shown in Figure 9-29.

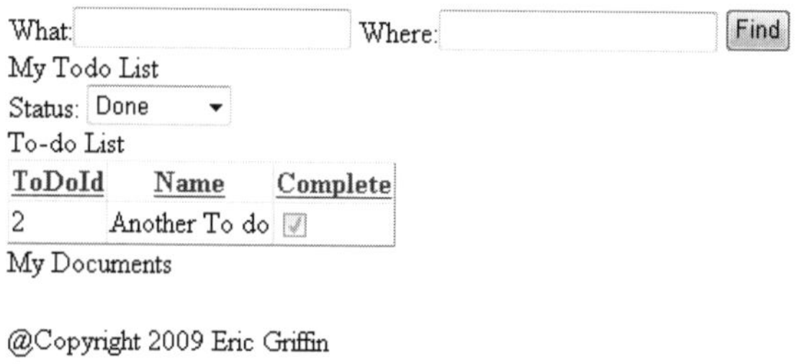

What: [_____]   Where: [_____] [Find]
My Todo List
Status: [Done   ▼]
To-do List

ToDoId	Name	Complete
2	Another To do	☑

My Documents

@Copyright 2009 Eric Griffin

Figure 9-29 *GridView* control displaying completed to-dos.

Editing Data with Data Controls

You can view completed and not completed to-dos, but you can't change the status. If you tried to click the check box in the Complete column, it would not respond. The ToDoId column should never be editable, but the *Name* field should be.

Let's add the ability to edit to-dos to the *GridView* control.

To edit data with the *GridView* control

1. Double-click **ToDoDataSet.xsd** to open the DataSet designer.

2. Right-click **ToTableAdapter** and select **Add Query**.

   The TableAdapter Query Configuration Wizard displays.

3. Select **Use SQL Statements**. Click **Next**.

   The next page asks you the type of query you want to create.

4. Select **UPDATE**. (See Figure 9-30.)

5. Click **Next**.

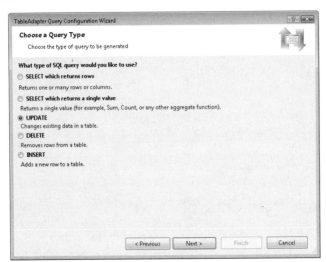

FIGURE 9-30 Creating an UPDATE query.

The next page enables you to define the SQL for the UPDATE statement. The default SQL statement does not have a table or query defined. (See Figure 9-31.)

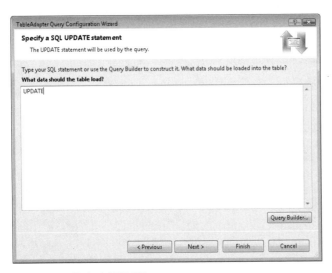

FIGURE 9-31 Default UPDATE query.

6. Click **Query Builder**.

   An error dialog box will appear because a table has not been defined in the query.

7. Click **OK** to close the dialog box.

8. Right-click the table pane at the top of **Query Builder**. Select **Add Table**.

   The Add Table dialog box displays.

9. Select the **ToDo** table from the Tables tab. Click **Add** to add the table to the Table pane. Click **Close**.

10. Select the **Name** and **Complete** columns. Notice that you cannot select the ToDoId column. This is not an updatable column, and the SQL has been added to the SQL pane, using the UPDATE SQL syntax:

```
UPDATE ToDo
SET Name =, Complete =
```

You must specify parameters for the Name and Complete columns.

11. Replace the existing query text with **SET Name = @Name, Complete = @Complete**.

```
UPDATE ToDo
SET Name = @Name, Complete = @Complete
```

UPDATE statements typically need a WHERE clause to limit the records it updates. If not, all the records will be updated to the same values. In this case, you want only one to-do to be updated at a time and, like your SELECT statement, you want to use a parameter to specify exactly which to-do should be updated. The ToDoId is the unique column to use.

12. Type **WHERE (ToDoId = @original_ToDoId)**.

```
UPDATE ToDo
SET Name = @Name, Complete = @Complete
WHERE (ToDoId = @original_ToDoId)
```

The ToDoId parameter is named this way specifically (original_<PrimaryKey>) because it is used by the ASP.NET data controls. More on this later. (See Figure 9-32.)

13. Click **OK** to close Query Builder.

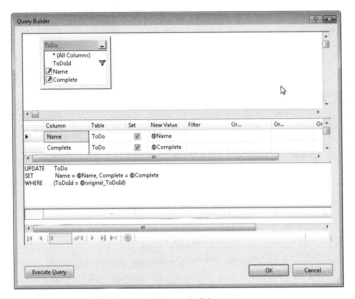

FIGURE 9-32 UPDATE query in Query Builder.

14. On the next page, leave the UpdateQuery default name of the function. (See Figure 9-33.) Click **Finish**.

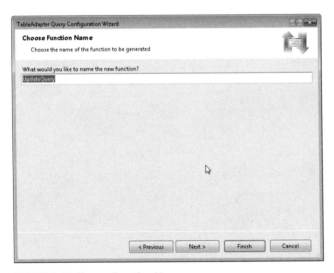

FIGURE 9-33 Choose Function Name.

Adding Editing to the *GridView* Control

Your data set and table adapter have been configured for updating data. Now you must enable it in the *GridView* control. Return to the Design view of the **Default.aspx** page.

To enable editing in a *GridView* control

1. Select the **ToDo GridView** control in the designer.

2. Click the configuration arrow and select **Edit Columns**.

   The Fields dialog box displays.

3. Scroll down to the Available Fields list and expand **CommandField**.

4. Select **Edit**, **Update**, **Cancel** and click **Add**. (See Figure 9-34.)

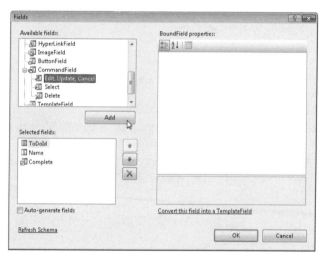

FIGURE 9-34 Selecting the Edit, Update, Cancel field.

5. With **Edit, Update, Cancel** selected in the Selected Fields list, click the **up arrow** to move the selection to the top of the list, above the **ToDoId**, **Name**, and **Complete** fields. (See Figure 9-35.)

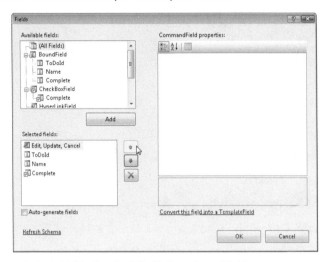

FIGURE 9-35 Moving the Edit, Update, Cancel field.

6. Click OK.

The *GridView* control now displays a new row with an Edit link beside each row. (See Figure 9-36.)

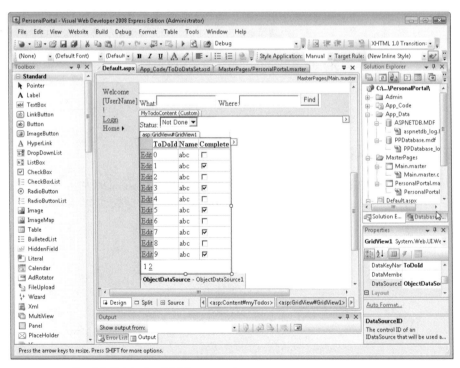

FIGURE 9-36 The Edit link in the *GridView* control.

7. Click the configuration arrow of **ObjectDataSource1** below the *GridView* control. Select **Configure Data Source**.

   The Configure Data Source dialog box displays.

8. Click the **UPDATE** tab. Select **UpdateQuery** from the Choose A Method drop-down menu. (See Figure 9-37.)

9. Click **Finish**.

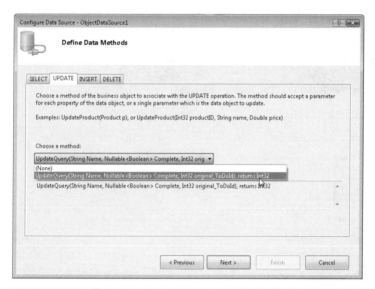

FIGURE 9-37 Configuring the data source to use the *UpdateQuery* method.

You've configured everything, so let's test it. Click **Run** on the standard toolbar. The browser opens the personal portal. After logging in, you can see your to-dos in the grid view. In this case, you have three to-dos, all completed. (See Figure 9-38.)

Let's change the first to-do to *Not Complete*. Click the **Edit** link by the first to-do. Two links appear: Update and Cancel. Also, the Name column has changed to an editable text box, and the check box is no longer dimmed.

Change the **Name** of the first to-do in the list and clear the **Complete** check box. (See Figure 9-39.)

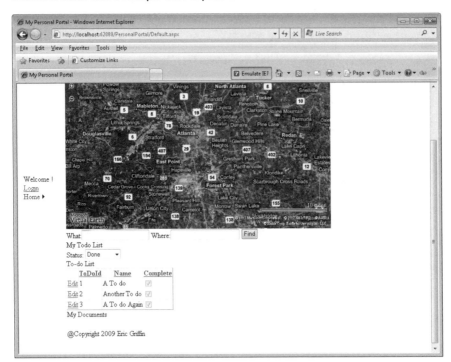

FIGURE 9-38 The personal portal with editable to-dos.

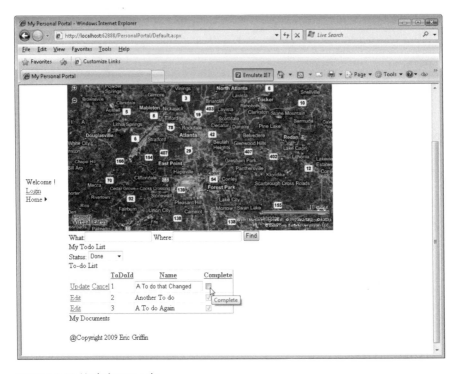

FIGURE 9-39 Updating a to-do.

Click **Update** to refresh the page and display only the two remaining complete to-dos. Select **Not Done** from the Status drop-down menu to see the changed to-do. (See Figure 9-40.) If you examine the *ToDo* database, you see that the row of the table has been changed.

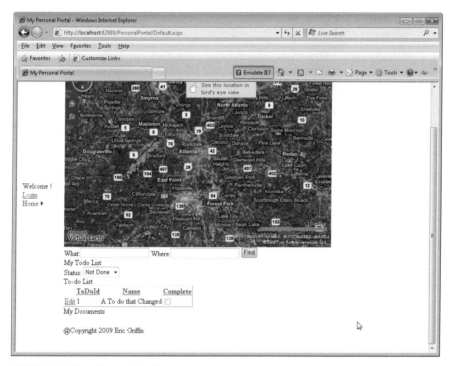

FIGURE 9-40 The changed to-do.

Adding New Data with Data Controls

After configuring the ability to edit to-dos, the only functionality you have left to configure is the ability to add to-dos. You will place the interface below the grid view. Switch to the Source view of **Default.aspx**. The add to-do functionality is facilitated by the *DetailsView* data control.

To add a *DetailsView* control

1. First, add a title to the section by using a <div> tag. Type the following below the *GridView* control markup in the Source view:

   ```
   <div>
     Add a New To-do
   </div>
   ```

2. Open the **Toolbox** if it is not open.

3. Scroll down to the **Data** section and expand it. Drag the *DataView* control from the Toolbox below the <div> tag for the title. The following markup is inserted.

```
<asp:DetailsView ID="DetailsView1" runat="server" Height="50px" Width="125px">
</asp:DetailsView>
```

4. Switch to the **Design** view to see the *DetailsView* control. (See Figure 9-41.)

5. Click **DetailsView** to select it.

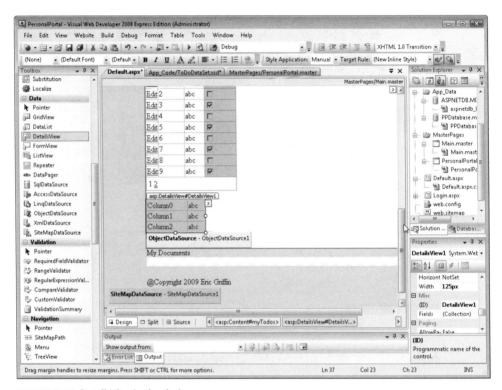

FIGURE 9-41 *DetailsView* in the designer.

6. In the Properties window, scroll to the **Behavior** section. You insert with *DetailsView* only, so set the DefaultMode property to insert from the drop-down list, as shown in Figure 9-42.

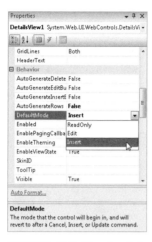

FIGURE 9-42 Setting the DefaultMode property.

That's all there is to configure. Click **Run**. The browser window displays the personal portal. Below the *GridView* control of to-dos, you see *DetailsView*.

Type some text of a new to-do in the **Name** text box. I typed "A new to do." Leave the Complete check box cleared. Click the **Insert** link to insert a new to-do. It should now display in the To-do List. (See Figure 9-43.)

FIGURE 9-43 Personal portal with editing and insertion of to-dos.

Summary

In this chapter, you learned how to create a data-driven user interface for to-dos in the personal portal. You learned how to create a data set and corresponding data tables to represent the *ToDo* database. You created queries in table adapters to retrieve and update data. You also learned how to use the grid view to display and edit to-dos and how to add new to-dos, using a *DetailsView* data control.

Chapter 10
Using Cascading Style

After completing this chapter, you will be able to

- Find Visual Web Developer Style windows.

- Attach a cascading style sheet to an ASP.NET page.

- Determine whether a style is assigned to an element.

- Find styles in a cascading style sheet.

- Apply styles to a *<div>* element.

- Apply styles to a table.

- Apply styles to a data view.

- Apply styles to a details view.

In the previous chapter, you learned about how Visual Web Developer can help you build data-driven Web interfaces. Another important aspect of interface design is the sites, colors, fonts, and element look and feel. Web-page look and feel can be customized and standardized, using cascading style sheets (CSS). In this chapter, I show you how you can create, use, and manage cascading style sheets in Visual Web Developer.

 Note The basics of CSS are easy to learn; creating sophisticated layouts with CSS takes a lot longer. Mastering CSS can take years of practice. The best way to learn more is to read the experts. I recommend the following two books to get you started and to help you understand the possibilities with CSS: *CSS Mastery: Advanced Web Standards Solutions*, by Andy Budd (Apress, 2006); and *The Zen of CSS Design: Visual Enlightenment for the Web*, by Dave Shea and Molly E. Holzschlag (Peachpit Press, 2005).

Cascading Style Sheets

Cascading style sheets simplify Hypertext Markup Language (HTML) by giving you the option of removing style markup and replacing it with style properties in a separate location. Examine the markup of a styled HTML <h1> element:

```
<h1><b><u><font face="arial" color="red">Hello World!</font></u></b></h1>
```

This markup creates a bold, underlined Hello World! in red Arial font. Imagine if, everywhere throughout your markup, you had to have extra markup for your pages' styles. Your page would be hard to follow and difficult to maintain. Enter CSS. Examine the same result, using CSS.

```
<h1 class="headline">Hello World!</h1>
```

Immediately, you can see how less cluttered the markup is. CSS uses the *class* attribute to specify a CSS selector to use to style the <h1> element. The *CSS* class would be defined in the style sheet as follows:

```
.headline
{
  text-decoration: underline;
  font-weight: bold;
  color: Red;
  font-family: Arial;
}
```

In CSS, styles are defined using selectors with properties separated by a semicolon. A CSS file can contain hundreds of selectors and can specify not only fonts and colors but absolute locations of HTML elements on a page.

Inline Styles

You can use inline styles directly in HTML markup by using the *style* attribute, but it can lead to the same problems as were mentioned in plain HTML. Using the preceding example:

```
<h1 style="text-decoration: underline; font-weight: bold; color: Red; font-family:
Arial;">Hello World!</h1>
```

Using Styles in Visual Web Developer

I have created a style sheet for the personal portal that is located in the source folder for Chapter 10 of this book's CD. It is called PersonalPortal.css.

Copy this file and the images folder into the PersonalPortal Web site directory in the Visual Studio 2008\Websites\PersonalPortal directory on your computer.

Add PersonalPortal.css to the project.

Style Management Windows

Visual Web Developer has three windows that help you use CSS. They are the CSS Properties, Manage Styles, and Apply Styles windows. They are available from the View menu when a style sheet is not selected in Solution Explorer. (See Figure 10-1.)

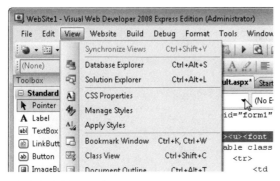

FIGURE 10-1 The style menus.

Select each one to open each window in the left section of the Visual Web Developer interface. Now you are ready to apply the styles in PersonalPortal.css. The master page is the natural place to start applying styles because all the styles applied to the master page will be applied to pages using it. For the personal portal, the parent master page is the PersonalPortal.master.

To apply styles to the master page

1. Open **PersonalPortal.master**. Select **Apply Styles**, using the tab at the bottom of the Visual Web Developer interface. (See Figure 10-2.)

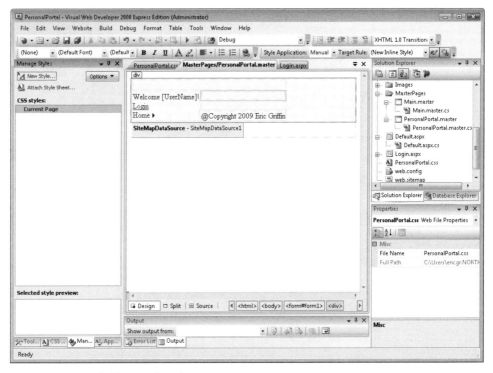

FIGURE 10-2 Unstyled PersonalPortal.master.

2. In the **Apply Styles** window, click **Attach Style Sheet**. (See Figure 10-3.)

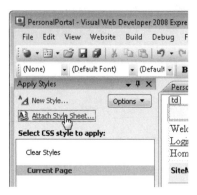

FIGURE 10-3 Clicking Attach Style Sheet.

The Select Style Sheet dialog box appears. The Project folders appear in the left-side list in the dialog box.

3. Select **PersonalPortal** at the top of the tree. Select **PersonalPortal.css** from the right-side list after it appears. Click **OK** to close the dialog box. (See Figure 10-4.)

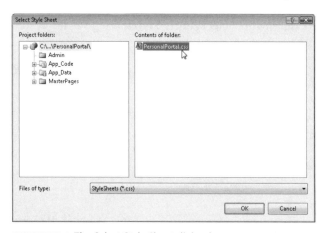

FIGURE 10-4 The Select Style Sheet dialog box.

When you return to Visual Web Developer, the PersonalPortal.master has changed color to a shade of blue. You will also see a list of items; some, with images, appear in the Apply Styles window. (See Figure 10-5.)

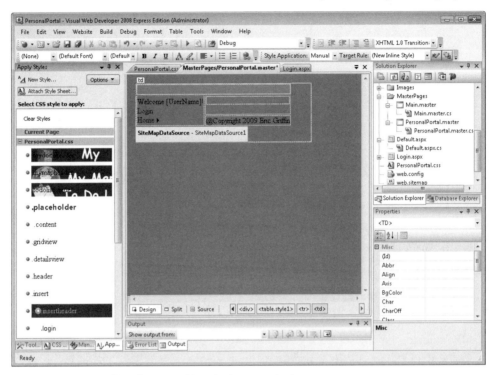

FIGURE 10-5 PersonalPortal.master with style sheet attached.

You know the style sheet was applied. How? Change to the Source view from the Design view for the PersonalPortal.master. Look in the *<head>* element at the top of the PersonalPortal.master, and you will find the following markup.

```
<link href="../PersonalPortal.css" rel="stylesheet" type="text/css" />
```

Visual Web Developer added this <link> reference. This is how you would attach the style sheet manually.

Now let's find out why the color changed to blue. Select the **Manage Styles** window while the PersonalPortal.master is open and active, using the tab at the bottom left of the Visual Web Developer interface.

This Manage Styles window provides a tree hierarchy view of all CSS selectors available from the current page. (See Figure 10-6.)

FIGURE 10-6 The Manage Styles window.

The selectors can be sorted (by element and type) and filtered (by current page or selection) using the Options button. (See Figure 10-7.)

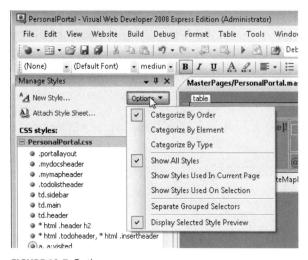

FIGURE 10-7 Options menu.

Each selector in the list has an icon to the left.

Style Selectors in Manage Styles

Icon	Style Type
Blue	Elements
Green	Classes
Red	IDs (used by HTML elements)
Grey circle	Style in use (color applies as shown)

You can see in the Manage Styles window that three styles are in use on PersonalPortal.master: a, form, and body, as shown in Figure 10-8.

FIGURE 10-8 Styles in use.

Every page has to have a body tag, and ASP.NET pages typically have a form. Hyperlinks are also common. Let's examine what's defined in the PersonalPortal.css.

Right-click the body selector. Select **Go To Code**.

The PersonalPortal.css file opens with the cursor set to the body selector. The following is defined:

```
body {
        background: #6B91C3;
        font: "Segoe UI", Segoe, sans-serif;
        margin: 0;
        padding: 18px;
        font-weight:bold;
        font-size:medium;
}
```

Notice the selector body. Because all HTML pages have a body, these styles will be applied by default. The background property is the value that set the color of the page. The value for colors is *Hex*. You can see several other styles are also set.

You can override this style for any elements contained in the <body> of the page by setting it to a different style that selects using IDs, styles, or classes.

Clearing Styles

The PersonalPortal.css styles I defined not only define colors and fonts but the table used to define the layout.

I have defined a style for the table used to lay out the Personal Portal interface. The style fixes the width and uses the *portallayout:* class. It is defined in PersonalPortal.css:

```
.portallayout
{
    width: 810px;
}
```

Let's start by setting styles. Before you start, it is a good idea to make sure you start with a clean slate. Clearing styles is the way to do this. Return to the **PersonalPortal.master** page in Design view. Examine the lower right corner of the designer to see that the table has a style already applied. (See Figure 10-9.) What is this?

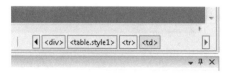

FIGURE 10-9 Table with a style created by Visual Web Developer.

Don't worry if you don't see this. It occurs only if you have adjusted the table or its rows or columns in the designer manually. Visual Web Developer creates a style on the fly to accommodate the exact change you made in the designer. You can find the defined style by switching to Code view. You might see code similar to this in the <head> section:

```
<style type="text/css">
    .style1
    {
        width: 136px;
    }
</style>
```

To clear a style of an element

1. Select the element in the designer or use the tag selector at the bottom of the designer to do so.

2. In the **Apply Styles** window, scroll to the top of the list and select **Clear Styles**. (See Figure 10-10.)

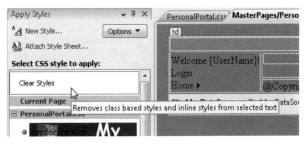

FIGURE 10-10 Selecting Clear Styles.

Setting Styles for the Personal Portal

Now that you have cleared the table of styles, you can apply the *portallayout* class to the table and the remaining styles to the layout.

To apply a style to a table

1. Select the **Personal Portal** table element in the designer or use the element selector to do so.

2. In the Apply Styles window, scroll to the *.portallayout* class in the list and select it or click the drop-down arrow and select **Apply Style**. (See Figure 10-11.)

FIGURE 10-11 Applying the portallayout style.

After the style is applied, the icon is circled in grey, indicating that it is applied for the table. The new width of the table in the designer is apparent. (See Figure 10-12.)

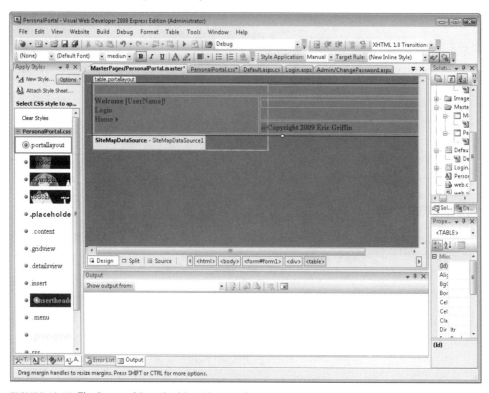

FIGURE 10-12 The Personal Portal table with portallayout style applied.

The next part of the table to style is the banner of the personal portal. I defined a class to be used with the <td> element of a table:

```
td.header
{
    height:174px;
    background-repeat: no-repeat;
    background-image: url(Images/blog-title.png);
}
```

I created an image called blog-title.png that I use with the style attribute's height to set the length of the table <td> to 174 px (the height of the image), background-repeat set to not repeat the image, and background-image set to the location of the image located in the *images* directory.

To set the style for the personal portal header

1. Click the top row of the personal portal layout table. (See Figure 10-13.)

FIGURE 10-13 Selecting the top row.

2. Scroll down in the Apply Styles window. Notice that there is a new section, called Contextual Selectors.

   This section will appear if you have selected an element in the designer that has a corresponding selector in the style sheet attached to the page. In this case, the <td> element is selected, so you see *td.header* and *td.sidebar* classes. (See Figure 10-14.)

FIGURE 10-14 Contextual Selectors in the Apply Styles window.

3. Click the **td.header** class in the Apply Styles window. (See Figure 10-15.)

FIGURE 10-15 Selecting the td.header style.

4. Select the <**td**> element in the designer that contains the *Login* controls.

   The class that you will apply to the element is defined here, called *td.sidebar*.

```
td.sidebar
{
    width: 200px;
    padding-left:10px;
    padding-top:10px;
}
```

5. In the Apply Styles window, select the **td.sidebar** class in the Contextual Selectors section. (See Figure 10-16.)

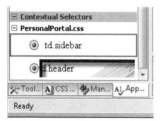

FIGURE 10-16 Selecting the td.sidebar style.

The result of applying both classes to the table <td> elements will look like Figure 10-17.

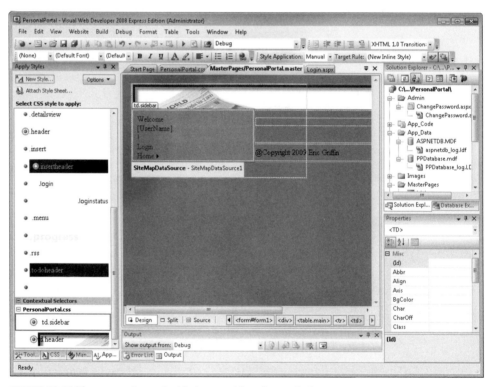

FIGURE 10-17 The personal portal table layout with styles applied.

Now that you have applied the styles, let's see what it looks like in the browser.

6. Click **Run**. The browser window opens to show the personal portal style changes. (See Figure 10-18.)

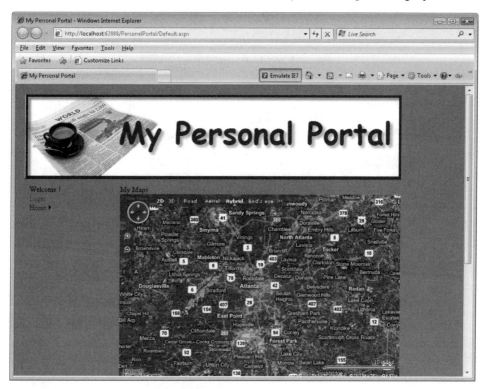

FIGURE 10-18 The styled personal portal running in a browser.

Setting the Personal Portal Header Styles

Let's move to the other areas that need styling, such as the headers for maps, to-dos, and documents. The sections are defined on the Main.master page. Open the **Main.master** in the Visual Web Developer designer. (See Figure 10-19.)

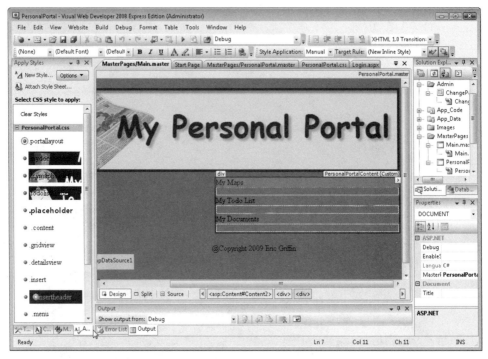

FIGURE 10-19 Unstyled Main.master.

You can see the changes to the PersonalPortal.master that have been applied to the Main. master. Switching to the **Source** view, the *PersonalPortalContent* content placeholder contains the *My Maps*, *My To-Dos*, and *My Documents* placeholders, as shown in Listing 10-1.

LISTING 10-1 *PersonalPortalContent* Content Placeholder

```
<asp:Content ID="Content2" ContentPlaceHolderID="PersonalPortalContent" Runat="Server">
  <div>
    <div class="mymapheader" ></div>
      <asp:contentplaceholder id="MyMapContent" runat="server"/>
    <div class="todolistheader" ></div>
      <asp:contentplaceholder id="MyTodoContent" runat="server"/>
    <div class="mydocsheader" ></div>
      <asp:contentplaceholder id="MyDocumentsContent" runat="server"/>
  </div>
</asp:Content>
```

I have defined classes in PersonalPortal.css to display an image for each header. The classes are *mymapheader*, *todolistheader*, and *mydocsheader*, respectively. (See Listing 10-2.)

LISTING 10-2 Header Styles in PersonalPortal.css

```
.mymapheader
{
    width: 210px;
    height: 66px;
    background-repeat: no-repeat;
```

```
        background-image: url(Images/mymapheader.png);
        padding-bottom: 10px;

}
.todolistheader
{
        width: 210px;
        height: 66px;
        background-repeat: no-repeat;
        background-image: url(Images/todobanner.png);
        padding-bottom: 10px;

}
.mydocsheader
{
        width: 254px;
        height: 66px;
        background-repeat: no-repeat;
        background-image: url(Images/mydocsheader.png);
        padding-bottom: 10px;
}
```

To set the styles for the header

1. Switch to **Design** view for the **Main.master**.

2. Click the words **My Map** to select the <**div**> element that contains the words.

3. In the Apply Styles windows, click the **mymapheader** class in the PersonalPortal.css section.

   The image mapheader.png should display with the words *My Map* appearing over it. (See Figure 10-20.)

FIGURE 10-20 Applying the mymapheader style.

4. Click the words **My Todo List** to select the **<div>** element that contains the words.

5. In the Apply Styles windows, click the **mytodoheader** class in the PersonalPortal.css section.

   The image todobanner.png displays with the words *My Todo List* appearing over it.

6. Click the words **My Documents** to select the **<div>** element that contains the words.

7. In the Apply Styles windows, click the **mydocsheader** class in the PersonalPortal.css section.

   The image mydocsheader.png displays with the words *My Documents* appearing over it.

8. Switch to **Source** view. Delete the **My Maps**, **My Todo List**, and **My Documents** text to keep them from appearing over the header images.

9. Look at the result in Figure 10-21.

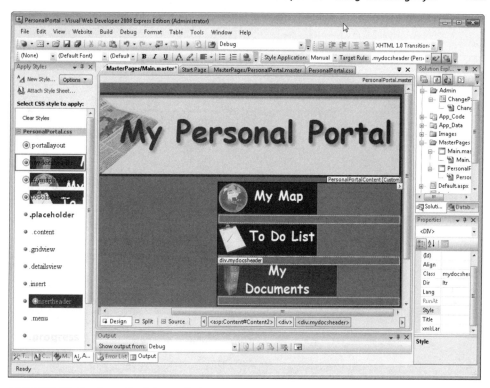

FIGURE 10-21 Headers with styles applied.

10. Click **Run**.

The browser window opens to show the Personal Portal style changes. (See Figure 10-22.)

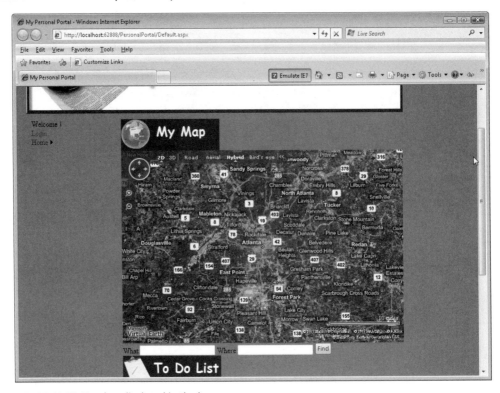

FIGURE 10-22 Headers displayed in the browser.

Setting Styles for the Data Interface Controls

The grids used by the To-do section of the personal portal that you created in the previous chapter also need styling. These controls are contained in the *Content* controls on the Default.aspx page. Open the **Default.aspx** page in the Visual Web Developer designer. Scroll down to the To-do data interface controls. (See Figure 10-23.)

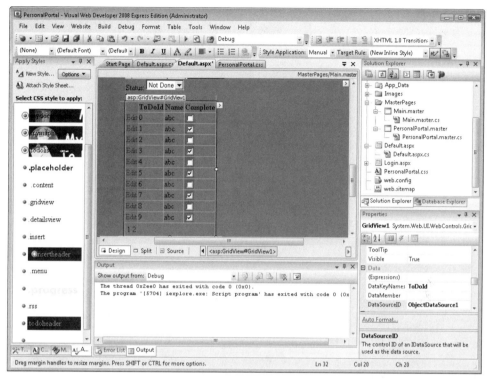

FIGURE 10-23 The unstyled grid view.

The Grid view is the first control that you style. Select **GridView** in the designer and switch to the Source view. The following markup will be highlighted. (See Listing 10-3.)

LISTING 10-3 *GridView* Markup

```
<div>
   To-do List
<div>
   <asp:GridView ID="GridView1" runat="server" AllowPaging="True"
      AllowSorting="True" AutoGenerateColumns="False"
      DataSourceID="ObjectDataSource1" DataKeyNames="ToDoId">
      <Columns>
         <asp:CommandField ShowEditButton="True" />
         <asp:BoundField DataField="ToDoId" HeaderText="ToDoId" InsertVisible="False"
            ReadOnly="True" SortExpression="ToDoId" />
         <asp:BoundField DataField="Name" HeaderText="Name" SortExpression="Name" />
         <asp:CheckBoxField DataField="Complete" HeaderText="Complete"
            SortExpression="Complete" />
      </Columns>
   </asp:GridView>
```

The markup represents the properties of the control. The control, at run time, generates a table with classes that can be used to style *GridView*. *GridView* styles I created in PersonalPortal.css are based on those classes, as Listing 10-4 shows.

LISTING 10-4 *GridView* Styles

```css
.todoheader
{
    color: Silver;
        background: #10377C;
        position: relative;
        font-weight:bold;
        font-size:medium;
}
.gridview .actions div {
        float: right;
        padding-right: 2px;
        text-align: right;
        width: 95px;
}

.gridview .edit td,.gridview .create td {
        background: #DAFFCD;
        padding: 4px;
        border-bottom: solid 2px #FFFFFF;
        border-top: solid 2px #FFFFFF;
}

.gridview td {
        background: #D7E6F4;
        border-bottom: solid 1px #C5DBF7;
        color: #333333;
        font: small "Segoe UI", Segoe, sans-serif;
        padding: 5px 4px;
}
.gridview td a{
        color: #0066CC;
        font: bold small "Segoe UI",Segoe,sans-serif;
        padding: 2px;
        text-decoration: none;
}
.gridview td a:hover {
        color: #333333;
        font-weight: bold;
}
.gridview th {
        background: #4168BD;
        color: #FFFFFF;
        font: small "Segoe UI", Segoe, sans-serif;
        letter-spacing: 0;
        padding: 4px;
        text-align: left;
}
.gridview th a{
        color: #FFFFFF;
        font: bold small "Segoe UI",Segoe,sans-serif;
}
.gridview th a:hover{
        color: #00FF00;
}
```

```
.gridview tr.even td,.detailsview tr.even td{
      background: #FFFFFF;
}
.gridview tr.header {
      background: #C5DBF7;
}
.gridview,.detailsview {
      width: 100%;
}
```

To style *GridView*

1. Select **GridView** in the designer.

2. Click the **gridview** class in the Apply Styles window.

   GridView becomes styled. (See Figure 10-24.)

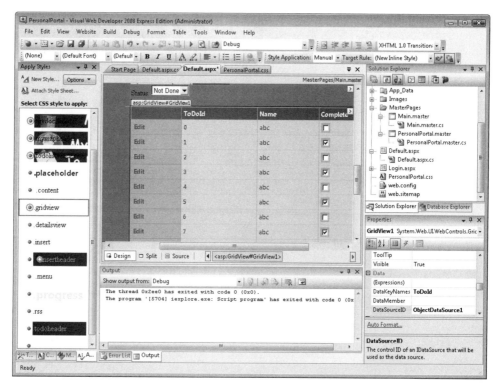

FIGURE 10-24 *GridView* with the *gridview* class attached.

3. Click the cursor inside the To-do List text to select the **<div>** that contains it.

4. Click the **todoheader** class in the Apply Styles window to set the style. (See Figure 10-25.)

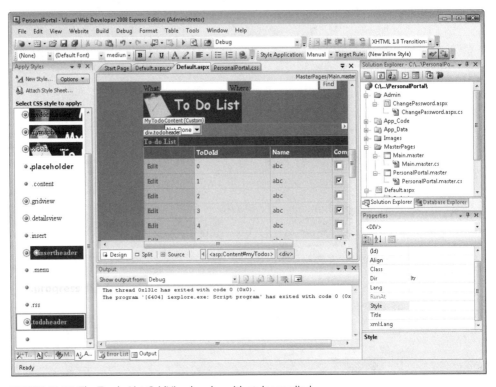

FIGURE 10-25 The To-do List *GridView* header with styles applied.

The *DetailsView* is the next control you style. Figure 10-26 shows the selected *DetailsView* control in Default.aspx.

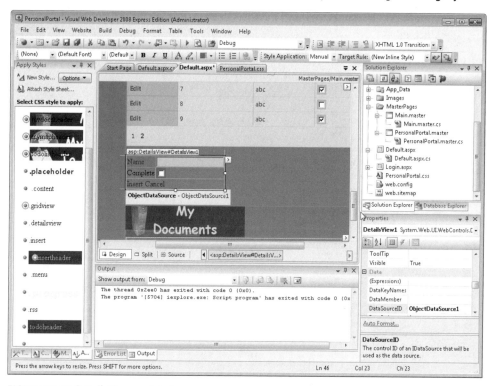

FIGURE 10-26 *DetailsView*, unstyled.

Select **DetailsView** in the designer and switch to the Source view. The following markup will be highlighted, as shown in Listing 10-5.

LISTING 10-5 *DetailsView* Markup

```
<div>
    Add a New To-do
</div>
<asp:DetailsView ID="DetailsView1" runat="server" Height="50px" Width="125px"
    AutoGenerateRows="False" DataSourceID="ObjectDataSource1"
    DefaultMode="Insert">
    <Fields>
        <asp:BoundField DataField="ToDoId" HeaderText="ToDoId" InsertVisible="False"
            ReadOnly="True" SortExpression="ToDoId" />
        <asp:BoundField DataField="Name" HeaderText="Name" SortExpression="Name" />
        <asp:CheckBoxField DataField="Complete" HeaderText="Complete"
            SortExpression="Complete" />
        <asp:CommandField ShowInsertButton="True" />
    </Fields>
</asp:DetailsView>
```

As with the *GridView* control, the *DetailsView* markup represents the properties of the control. The control, at run time, generates a table with classes that can be used to style

DetailsView. The *DetailsView* styles I created in PersonalPortal.css are based on those classes. (See Listing 10-6.)

LISTING 10-6 *DetailsView* Styles

```css
.insertheader
{
    color: Silver;
        background: #10377C url(images/add.gif) 6px 50% no-repeat;
        margin-top: 25px;
        padding-left: 25px;
        position: relative;
        font-size:medium;
        width:125px;
    font-weight:bold;
}
.detailsview .actions div {
        float: right;
        text-align: right;
        width: 95px;
        padding-right: 2px;
}
.detailsview td {
        background: #D7E6F4;
        color: #333333;
        font: small "Segoe UI", Segoe, sans-serif;
        padding: 15px 10px 10px 10px;
}
.detailsview td a {
        color: #0066CC;
        font: bold small "Segoe UI", Segoe, sans-serif;
        padding-right: 10px;
}
.detailsview td a:hover {
        font-weight: bold;
        color: #333;
}
.detailsview th {
        background: #4168BD;
        color: #FFFFFF;
        font: small "Segoe UI", Segoe, sans-serif;
        letter-spacing: 0;
        padding: 3px 8px 5px;
        padding: 2px;
        text-align: left;
}
.detailsview tr.header {
        background: #C5DBF7;
        padding: 3px 8px 5px;
}
```

To style *DetailsView*

1. Select **DetailsView** in the designer.

2. Click the **detailsview** class in the Apply Styles window.

   DetailsView becomes styled. (See Figure 10-27.)

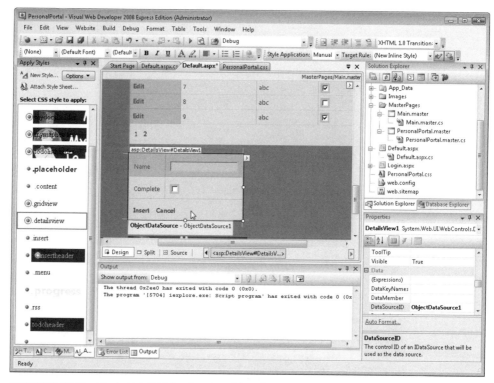

FIGURE 10-27 The To-do List *GridView* header with styles applied.

3. Place the cursor inside the Add A New To-Do text to select the **<div>** that contains it.

4. Click the **insertheader** class in the Apply Styles window to set the style. (See Figure 10-28.)

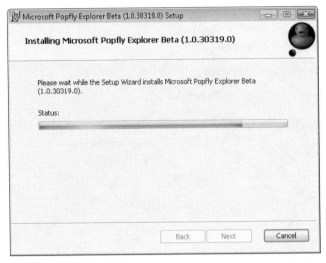

FIGURE 10-28 The To-do List *GridView* header with styles applied.

5. To see all the changes, click **Run**.

 The browser window opens to show the personal portal style changes. (See Figure 10-29.)

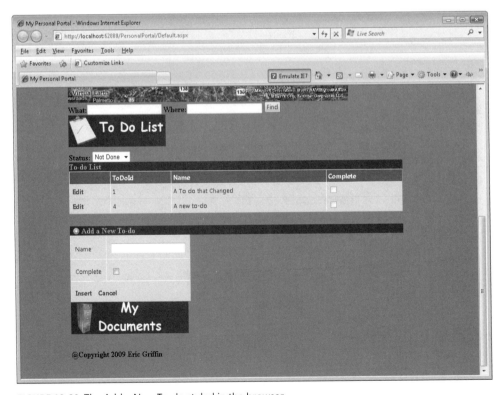

FIGURE 10-29 The Add a New To-do styled in the browser.

Summary

In this chapter, you learned about cascading style sheets (CSS) and how to attach an existing style sheet to an ASP.NET page. You learned how to find the definition of styles and how to apply the style to an element. You styled the personal portal by using a style sheet to display a banner and section headers with an image, and you styled the data interface controls.

Chapter 11
Understanding and Using Mashups

After completing this chapter, you will be able to

- Explain what a mashup is.
- Explain what Popfly is and how to create an account.
- Use Popfly blocks to create mashup functionality.
- Test a Popfly mashup.
- Install Popfly Explorer.
- Embed Popfly mashups in ASP.NET pages.
- Tweak a Popfly mashup after it has been embedded.

In the previous chapter, you learned how to use cascading style sheets to style the personal portal. If you refer back to the requirements of your persona, Eric, they state that he likes to read RSS feeds to stay up with news. In this chapter, you add functionality to the personal portal to enable Eric to read news about his home city, Atlanta.

Introducing Mashups

You use a new technology, called mashups, to accomplish this. A mashup is software that combines, mixes, and "mashes" application programming interfaces (APIs) and data sources from different companies to create something new. (See Figure 11-1.)

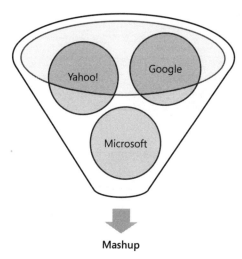

Mashup

FIGURE 11-1 A mashup.

As with many of the technologies I have shown you in this book, other books delve deeper into mashups. One book is by a author I know personally: *Foundations of Popfly: Rapid Mashup Development*, by Eric Griffin (Apress, 2008). Another good reference is *Pro Web 2.0 Mashups: Remixing Data and Web Services*, by Raymond Yee (Apress, 2008).

Popfly

Visual Web Developer is a tool for creating Web applications, not mashups. However, it does integrate with a tool designed specifically to enable you to create mashups quickly and with little or no programming. It is called Microsoft Popfly (*http://www.popfly.com*). (See Figure 11-2.)

FIGURE 11-2 Microsoft Popfly Web site.

Popfly was introduced in May 2007. It was created to enable nonprofessional programmers to create mashups without having to write a line of code. It is also an online community that enables its members to rate and share mashups with other community members.

Silverlight

Microsoft Popfly is built with another hot technology, called Silverlight. Microsoft Silverlight is a cross-browser, cross-platform, and cross-device plug-in for delivering the next generation of .NET-based media experiences and rich interactive applications for the Web. It is required for the use of Popfly and can be downloaded and installed at *http://silverlight.net/*.

To create a new Popfly account

1. After you have installed Silverlight, visit **http://www.popfly.com**.

2. Click the **Windows Live Sign In** icon on the Popfly home page.

   The browser navigates to the **Windows Live** login. (See Figure 11-3.)

 Note If you don't have a Windows Live ID, click Sign Up and follow the guided process. Then return to step 1.

FIGURE 11-3 Windows Live login.

3. Sign In by typing your password.

   The browser navigates to the Create Your Profile page. (See Figure 11-4.)

4. Type a user name to use in the Popfly community. Optionally, choose an avatar image or upload one. Read the Terms of Use agreement and click **I Agree**.

FIGURE 11-4 Create Your Profile page.

Creating Your First Mashup

After you create your profile, you are returned to the main Popfly page, which offers you the option to Create A Game, Create A Mashup, or Create A Web Page. You can also browse through the mashups that others have created using Popfly by exploring the Popfly community through the Featured Projects, Top Rated Projects, Newest Projects, and Top Users tabs near the bottom half of the page. (See Figure 11-5.)

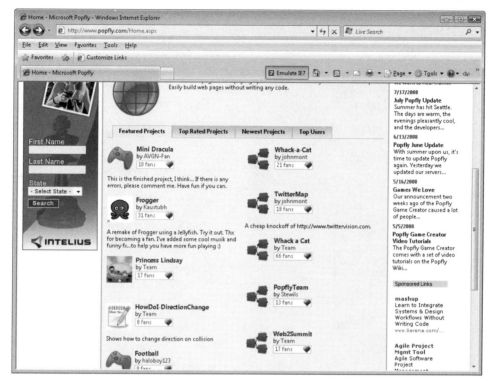

FIGURE 11-5 Exploring other mashups.

After you have looked at a few mashups created by other users, you can start creating one of your own.

To create your first mashup

1. Select **Mashup** from the **Create** menu.

   The Popfly mashup designer appears in Edit mode. The Edit menu is the largest item; Html and Run are the two other major options. The Blocks pane contains the components, or *blocks* used to create mashups. More on that shortly. Help is available from the pane on the right side of the page. (See Figure 11-6.)

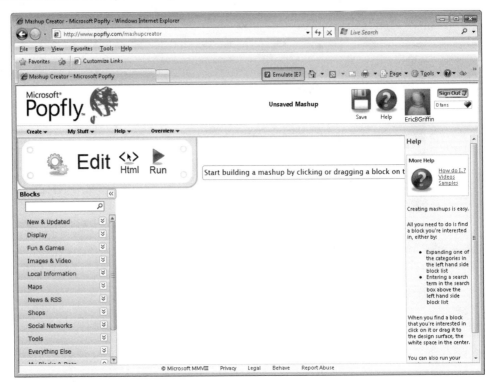

FIGURE 11-6 The Popfly mashup designer.

2. Press **Run** to see the environment change into Run mode.

   The Run button is now the largest. Notice that Help and the blocks panes have disappeared and, because you haven't done anything yet, the preview pane is blank. (See Figure 11-7.)

FIGURE 11-7 Popfly designer in Run mode.

3. Click **Edit** to return to Edit mode. Click the **News & RSS** section of the **Blocks** pane to expand it. (See Figure 11-8.)

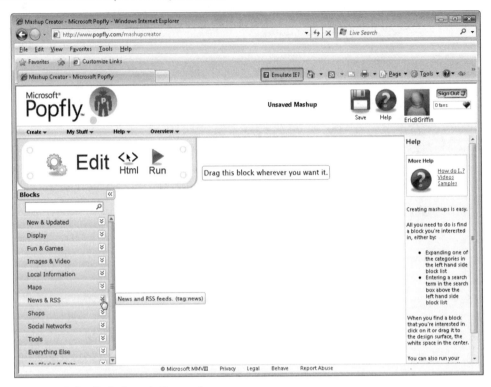

FIGURE 11-8 Popfly designer in Run mode.

4. Drag the **Live News** block onto the designer surface. (See Figure 11-9.)

After the Live News block is on the surface, you can see a tip displayed giving you an overview of the Live News block's Operation: Search and some of its parameters (for example, Query and Count). You also see a pink alert stating Missing Key. (See Figure 11-10.)

Note Many blocks are services created by vendors that want to track usage of their service by developers. Live News, a service by Microsoft, requires a unique key to use it.

FIGURE 11-9 Dragging Live News.

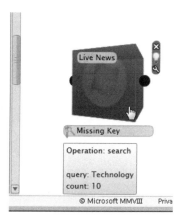

FIGURE 11-10 The Live News block.

5. Click the **Missing Key** alert to open a Windows Live News Search key dialog box.

   Because you don't have a Windows Live News Search key, click the related link. (See Figure 11-11.)

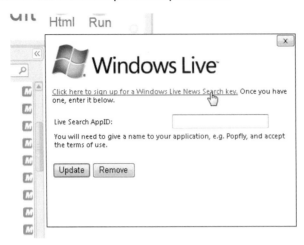

FIGURE 11-11 Windows Live News Search key dialog box.

A new browser window opens to the Live Search Developer Center.

6. Enter your personal name in the **Company Name** field on the page. (See Figure 11-12.)

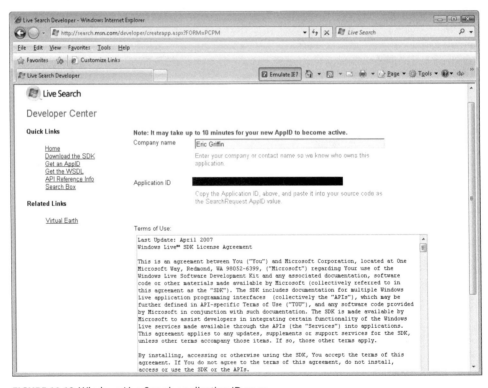

FIGURE 11-12 Windows Live Search application ID page.

7. Copy the **Application ID** onto the clipboard. Click **I Agree** after reading the terms of use of the service.

8. Close the window and return to the Windows Live News Search key dialog box.

9. Paste the application ID from the clipboard into the **AppID** field in the dialog box. Click **Update**. (See Figure 11-13.)

FIGURE 11-13 Updating the application ID.

The alert changes to green, indicating that the application key has been successfully entered. (See Figure 11-14.)

FIGURE 11-14 Live News block with an application key.

10. Click the **wrench** icon.

The Live News configuration screen displays, showing the Live News operations (search and total number of results).

11. Leave the default at Search. Type **Atlanta** in the **Query** value field. Enter **20** in the **Count** value field. (See Figure 11-15.)

FIGURE 11-15 Live News block configuration view.

12. To see what's going on behind the scenes, click **Switch to an advanced view** to display the JavaScript used by the block. (See Figure 11-16.)

The following JavaScript is displayed and can be edited:

```
liveNews.__reserved.pendingCalls = 1;
liveNews.search("Atlanta", 20, function(result)
    {
        try
        {
            data["Live News"] = result;

            checkForCallingDepth1();
        }
        catch (ex)
        {
            environment.reportError(ex);
            checkForCallingDepth1();
        }
    }
);
```

FIGURE 11-16 Live News block advanced configuration view.

13. Switch back to the default configuration view by clicking **Go back to simple view**. Drag a News Reader block from the **News & RSS** section of the **Blocks** pane. (See Figure 11-17.)

FIGURE 11-17 A new News Reader block on the design surface.

14. Click the sphere to the right side of the **Live News** block to begin a link arrow.

The News Reader sphere on its left side should enlarge and turn orange. (See Figure 11-18.)

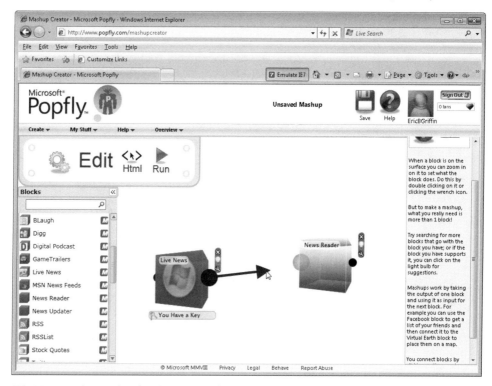

FIGURE 11-18 Connecting the Live News and News Reader blocks.

15. Click the **News Reader** sphere to connect the two blocks.

The two blocks are now connected. (See Figure 11-19.)

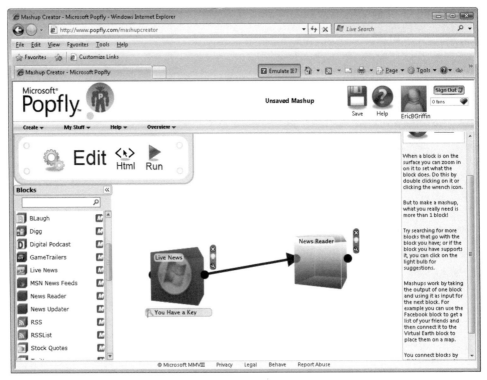

FIGURE 11-19 Connected Live News and News Reader blocks.

16. Click the **wrench** icon of the News Reader.

    When the News Reader configuration view displays, you can see that it has already rec-ognized the Live News as an input and its fields, *title*, *description*, *url*, *displayUrl*, *source*, and *totalCount*. Live News **title** is assigned to the headline, **date** is left blank, *content* is set to **description**, and *fullstoryUrl* is set to **url**.

17. Type **Eric's News** in the *title* field of the Properties section. (See Figure 11-20.)

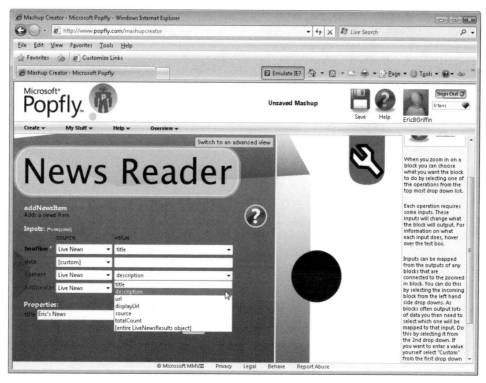

FIGURE 11-20 Connected Live News and News Reader blocks.

18. Click the **wrench** to exit the configuration view.

19. Click **Run** to view the mashup. (See Figure 11-21.)

    You can scroll through the news pulled from the Live News search by using the arrows at the bottom of the display. If you click the title of the news item, it will open a new window that shows the source of the news.

FIGURE 11-21 Eric's News running in Popfly.

Now you must save the mashup.

20. Click **Edit** to return to the designer. Click **Save**.

21. Type **My News** as the name of the mashup. Click **Accept**, and then click **Save**. (See Figure 11-22.)

FIGURE 11-22 Saving the My News mashup.

Visual Web Developer and Popfly

Visual Web Developer is integrated with Popfly by using Popfly Explorer, a Visual Web Developer add-in that enables you to access your Popfly projects and use them within the Visual Web Developer integrated developer environment.

To install Popfly Explorer

1. Download **Popfly Explorer** from **http://popfly.com/Overview/Explorer.aspx** to a location on your computer. (See Figure 11-23.)

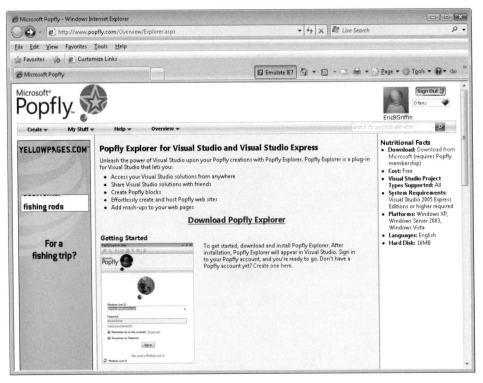

FIGURE 11-23 The Popfly Explorer download page.

2. With Visual Web Developer not running, execute the installation executable.

In this case, it is called **PopflyExplorerBeta.exe** from the location where you saved it. The first step in the installation displays. (See Figure 11-24.)

FIGURE 11-24 The Popfly Explorer setup step 1.

3. Click **Next**.

The next step is the End User License Agreement.

4. Read it and, if you agree, select **I accept the terms of the License Agreement**. (See Figure 11-25.) Click **Next**.

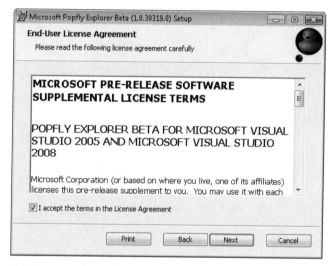

FIGURE 11-25 The Popfly Explorer Setup License Agreement.

You can change the location of the installation by using the Change button, or you can accept the default location. (See Figure 11-26.)

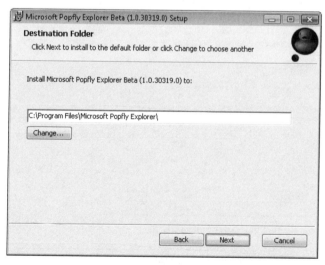

FIGURE 11-26 Setting the Popfly Explorer Destination Folder.

5. Click **Next**.

Popfly Explorer is ready to install with the next step. (See Figure 11-27.)

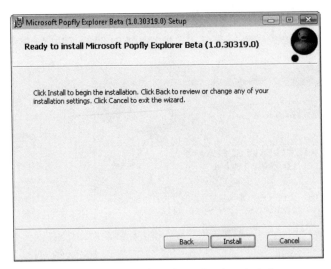

FIGURE 11-27 The Popfly Explorer Setup Ready to Install page.

6. Click **Install**.

   The Install progress step appears. Wait until the Next button becomes enabled. (See Figure 11-28.)

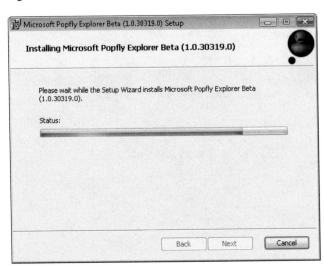

FIGURE 11-28 The Popfly Explorer Setup Progress page.

7. After the installation has completed, click **Finish**. See Figure 11-29.

FIGURE 11-29 The Finish page of Popfly Explorer setup.

Using Popfly Explorer

After Popfly Explorer is installed, you can use it within Visual Web Developer. Start **Visual Web Developer**. Notice that a new menu called Popfly displays. Select **Show Popfly Explorer** from the **Popfly** menu. (See Figure 11-30.)

FIGURE 11-30 Show Popfly Explorer.

A Popfly Explorer tab appears with Solution Explorer and Database Explorer tabs. Click the Popfly Explorer tab to start Popfly Explorer. You might see a message stating "Connecting to Popfly Explorer service, please wait." (See Figure 11-31.)

FIGURE 11-31 The Popfly Explorer starting up.

After connecting, you are presented with a Windows Live ID Sign In window. Type your Windows Live ID and password in the respective fields and click **Sign In**. (See Figure 11-32.)

FIGURE 11-32 The Popfly Explorer Windows Live ID Sign In window.

After a few seconds, you are presented with your data from the Popfly site. There is a folder for your projects (in which you should see your My News project) and a Friends folder. At the top of the explorer is a command bar with buttons. (See Figure 11-33.)

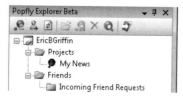

FIGURE 11-33 The Popfly Explorer

From left to right on this command toolbar, the following icons appear:

View My Popfly Page
Clicking this icon opens a Web browser to your Popfly page in a Web browser.

Add a Friend
Clicking this icon opens a dialog box to search and select new friends you want to add.

Refresh
Clicking this icon reconnects to the Popfly service and shows any new changes to your Popfly environment.

Open Project
Clicking this icon opens a selected project if you have saved your Visual Web Developer projects to the Popfly environment.

Save To Popfly
Clicking this button enables you to save the current open project to the Popfly environment.

Delete from Popfly
Clicking this icon enables you to delete the selected item from the Popfly environment.

Find Project
Clicking this icon enables you to search for projects shared by other Popfly users.

Sign Out
Clicking this icon signs you out of the Popfly environment.

Embedding Mashups in ASP.NET Pages

To embed the My News Popfly mashup

1. Start **Visual Web Developer** and open the **PersonalPortal** project. Click the **Solution Explorer** tab and open the **PersonalPortal.master** in the designer.

2. Click the **Popfly Explorer** tab. Sign on to Popfly, using your Windows Live ID. Open the **Projects** folder to find the **My News** mashup.

3. Drag the **My News** mashup from **Poplfy Explorer** to the **Personal Portal** table cell below the site's menu. (See Figure 11-34.)

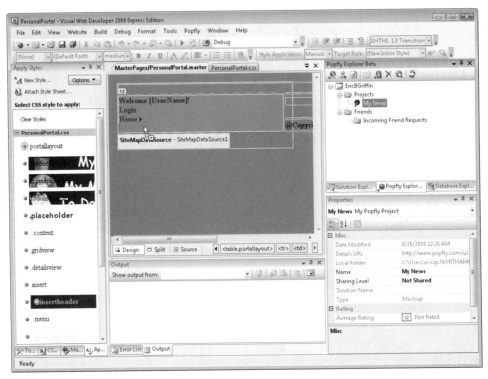

FIGURE 11-34 Dragging the My News mashup to the PersonalPortal table layout.

A dialog box will appear, stating that the My News mashup is not shared.

4. Click **Yes** to share it. (See Figure 11-35.)

FIGURE 11-35 Do You Want To Share Mashup dialog box.

5. Resize the placeholder for the mashup by using the mouse on its borders to be a width of **197** pixels and a height of **276** pixels.

Listing 1 shows the code of the frame that was created when you dragged the mashup to the PersonalPortal.master. (See Figure 11-36.)

LISTING 11-1 Popfly Mashup Frame

```
<iframe id="I1" allowtransparency="true" frameborder="no" name="I1"

  src="http://www.popfly.com/users/[YOURACCOUNTNAME]My%20News.small"

  style="background: #6B91C3;width: 197px; height: 276px"></iframe>
```

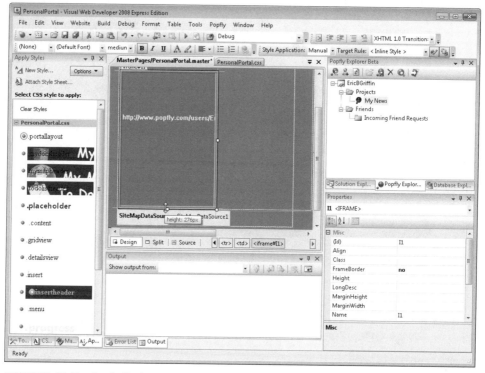

FIGURE 11-36 The Popfly Explorer Setup ready to install.

6. To see the results, click **Run**.

The browser will open and load the My News mashup. The latest RSS news is retrieved and displayed. Clicking the title of the news item navigates the browser to the article. Clicking the Next button displays the next article summary. (See Figure 11-37.)

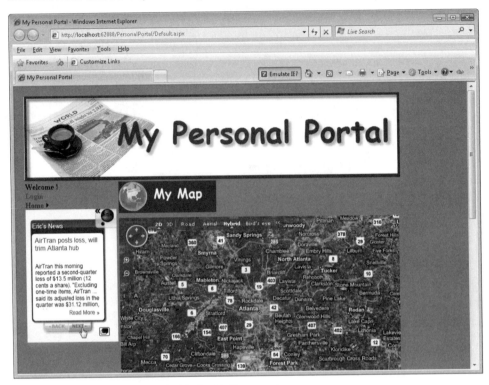

FIGURE 11-37 The Personal Portal with the My News mashup.

Tweaking Your Mashup

One thing you might notice is that the mashup stands out because of the white background. It would be better if the background matched the Personal Portal background. You can do that in Popfly by tweaking the mashup.

To tweak your mashup

1. Sign on to the Popfly Web site at **http://popfly.com**. Select **Projects** from the **My Stuff** menu, and then select the **My News** mashup.

2. Click the **Tweak This** link. (See Figure 11-38.)

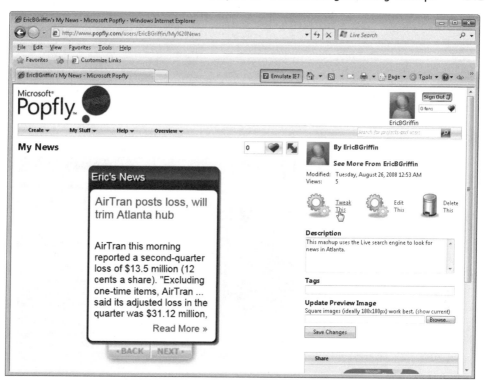

FIGURE 11-38 Tweaking the My News mashup.

3. Click **preferredBackgroundColor** and select a color close to the personal portal color. (See Figure 11-39.)

   (Unfortunately, at the time of writing, you can't enter the exact color using hex; the color of the personal portal is a shade of blue represented by #6B91C3.)

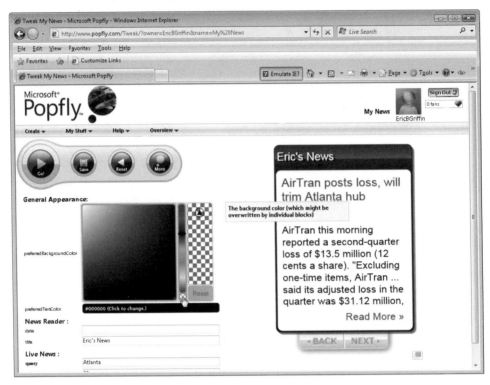

FIGURE 11-39 Editing the MyNews Popfly mashup.

4. Click **Go** to preview the color. Click **Save** when you are satisfied.

5. To see the results, run the personal portal again from **Visual Web Developer**.

   The browser opens to show the new background color of the My News mashup. (See Figure 11-40.)

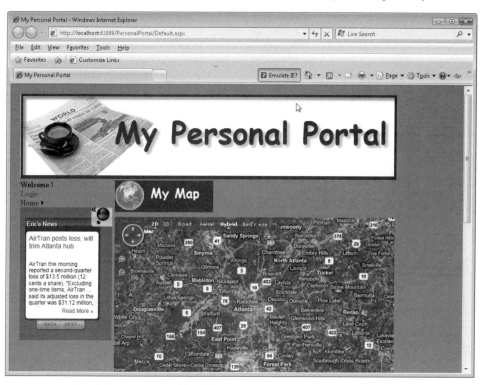

FIGURE 11-40 Tweaked My News mashup running in the personal portal.

Summary

In this chapter, you learned about mashups, small programs that integrate APIs and data from different and sometimes competing companies. Popfly is the new mashup-creation software that enables you to create mashups quickly and without coding. Popfly Explorer, a Visual Web Developer add-in, enables you to embed mashups in ASP.NET pages.

Chapter 12
Working with Web Services

After completing this chapter, you will be able to

- Use the File Upload control in a page.

- Upload documents to a location on the server.

- Create a Web service.

- Reference a Web service in your project.

- Use a Web service in an ASP.NET page.

In the previous chapter, you learned about mashups, how to create them in Microsoft Popfly, and how to integrate them in ASP.NET pages, using Visual Web Developer. Mashups combine, or mash, Web services from different vendors to create new applications.

In this chapter, you learn how to create your own Web service with Visual Web Developer. The service will help create new functionality in uploading and accessing documents for the personal portal.

Uploading Files to the Server

One of the important features your user, Eric, would like is to have his documents available through the personal portal. He travels and is frequently consulting from a client's site, so he would like to have access to his files from a public terminal or one of his client's computers.

To build this functionality, you need to create a location on the Web site to store the documents. Open **Visual Web Developer** and open the **Personal Portal** project.

Right-click the Personal Portal project in **Solution Explorer**. Select **New Folder**. Type **MyDocuments** as the name of the folder. (See Figure 12-1.)

FIGURE 12-1 The created MyDocuments folder.

You can use the ASP.NET *FileUpload* control to upload files from a Web page. You will add it to the My Documents section of the personal portal.

To add the *FileUpload* control to a Web page

1. Open the Default.aspx page.

   The personal portal uses two master pages to define the layout of all its Web pages. The best place to locate the control is on the **Default.aspx** page within the **MyDocumentsContent** area.

2. Open the toolbox and expand the **Standard** section. Drag the **FileUpload** control to the **MyDocumentContents** area. (See Figure 12-2.)

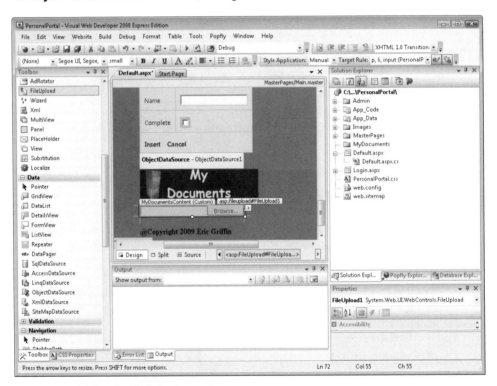

FIGURE 12-2 Adding the *FileUpload* control.

3. Change from Design to **Source** view.

   The code should look like Listing 12-1.

   LISTING 12-1 CONTENT CONTROL WITH *FILEUPLOAD*

```
<asp:Content ID="Content2" runat="server" contentplaceholderid="MyDocumentsContent">
  <asp:FileUpload ID="FileUpload1" runat="server" />
</asp:Content>
```

4. Type **
** (an HTML line break) after the *FileUpload* control markup and press Enter to advance to the next line.

5. Drag a **Button** control from the **Standard** section to the new line under **FileUpload** and line break. Type **"BtnUpload"** as the value for the *ID* attribute and **"Upload"** as the value for the *Text* attribute. The code should look like Listing 12-2.

LISTING 12-2 CONTENT CONTROL WITH *FILEUPLOAD* AND BUTTON

```
<asp:Content ID="Content2" runat="server" contentplaceholderid="MyDocumentsContent">
    <asp:FileUpload ID="FileUpload1" runat="server" /><br />
        <asp:Button ID="BtnUpload" runat="server" Text="Upload"/>
</asp:Content>
```

6. Switch back to **Design** view to see the button located underneath the *FileUpload* control. (See Figure 12-3.)

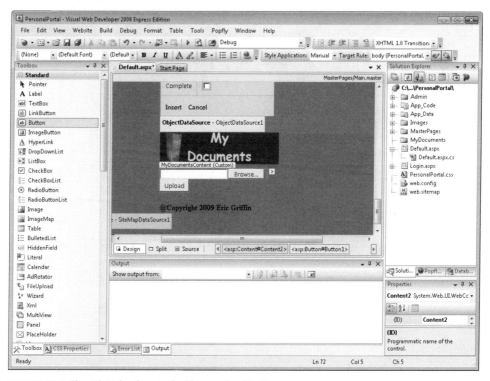

FIGURE 12-3 The *FileUpload* control with an upload button.

7. To see how the control behaves on a Web page, click **Run** on the standard toolbar.

   The browser opens to the personal portal.

8. Scroll down to the bottom of the personal portal. (See Figure 12-4.)

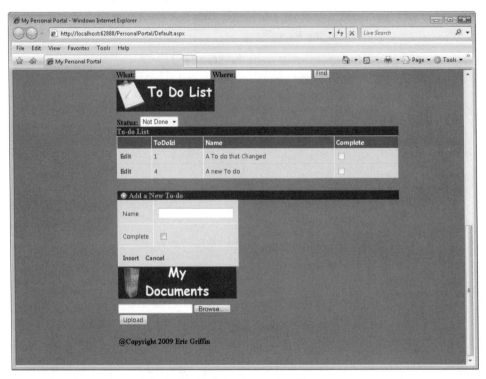

FIGURE 12-4 Personal portal displaying *FileUpload* control and button.

9. Click **Browse**.

A Choose File dialog box displays, enabling you to choose a file from your file system. (See Figure 12-5.)

10. Select a file from your hard drive. Click **Open**.

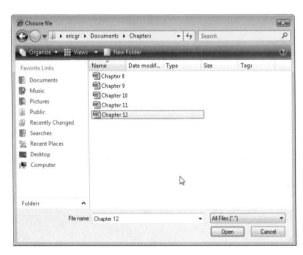

FIGURE 12-5 Selecting a file.

The dialog box closes, and the filename appears in the text box. (See Figure 12-6.)

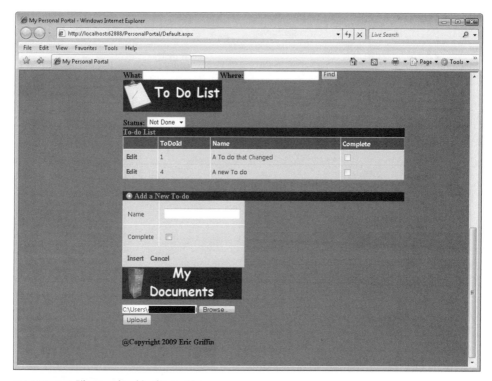

FIGURE 12-6 File to upload in the text box.

If you click **Upload**, nothing will happen. You must program the *FileUpload* control to upload the file to the MyDocuments folder on your site.

Programming the *FileUpload* Control

Stop running the personal portal. Return to the **Design** view of the **Default.aspx** page. Double-click **Upload**. Visual Web Developer opens the corresponding Microsoft Visual C# code-behind file called Default.aspx.cs. A new method has been created called *BtnUpload_Click* automatically for you. (See Figure 12-7.)

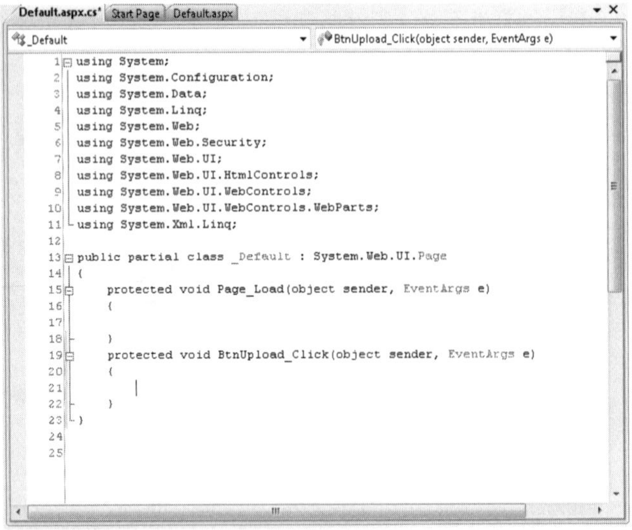

FIGURE 12-7 New *BtnUpload_Click* method.

Type the code in Listing 12-3 into the *BtnUpload_Click* method.

LISTING 12-3 *BtnUpload_Click* Code

```
if (this.FileUpload1.HasFile)
{
    string filename = Server.MapPath("~/Mydocuments") + "\\" + this.FileUpload1.FileName;
    this.FileUpload1.SaveAs(filename);
}
```

The code first tests that the *FileUpload* control has a valid file by using the *HasFile* method. If the value is true, a string variable is created to hold a constructed value for the file that will be created on the server. This is done using the *Server.MapPath* method, which determines the file path of the MyDocuments directory. This needs to be dynamic because if you deploy the personal portal on a remote server, you might not have the actual server drive locations. The mapped path for the MyDocuments folder is combined with the file name of the document that is parsed from the text box. Now that the complete path for the uploaded file has been created, the next line uses the *SaveAs* method to copy and create the file in the MyDocuments directory.

Repeat the steps earlier in this chapter. This time, the Upload button will execute the code you added. Each file you upload should be displayed in Solution Explorer. In the case of Figure 12-8, the Chapter12.docx file was uploaded.

Note You might have to refresh the contents of Solution Explorer to see uploaded documents in the MyDocuments folder.

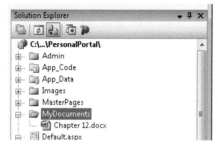

FIGURE 12-8 Chapter12.docx uploaded to the server.

Creating a Web Service

Now that you can upload files to the server, you need a way to see and download the files that have been uploaded. You use a Web service to accomplish it. The Web service enumerates the number of files located on the server and provides a list you can display in the MyDocuments section of the personal portal. The list will be links that, when clicked, will download the file.

To add a Web service to the project

1. Right-click the personal portal project in **Solution Explorer**. Select **Add New Item**.

   The Add New dialog box displays.

2. Select **Web Service** from the **Templates** list and type **MyDocuments.asmx** in the **Name** text box. (See Figure 12-9.)

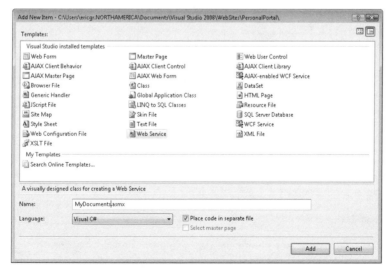

FIGURE 12-9 Add New Item dialog box.

3. Click **Add**.

   Two objects are added to the personal portal project: MyDocuments.cs in the App_Code folder, representing the C# code for the Web service, and MyDocuments.asmx, which holds the Web interface of the Web service. (See Figure 12-10.)

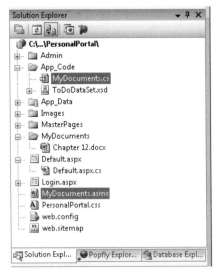

FIGURE 12-10 Web Service components.

4. Double-click **MyDocuments.cs** in **Solution Explorer** to open the default C# code.

   The code should look like Listing 12-4.

   LISTING 12–4 Default C# Code Created in MyDocuments.cs

```
using System;
using System.Collections.Generic;
using System.Linq;
using System.Web;
using System.Web.Services;
/// <summary>
/// Summary description for MyDocuments
/// </summary>
[WebService(Namespace = "http://tempuri.org/")]
[WebServiceBinding(ConformsTo = WsiProfiles.BasicProfile1_1)]
// To allow this Web Service to be called from script, using ASP.NET AJAX, uncomment
the following line.
// [System.Web.Script.Services.ScriptService]
public class MyDocuments : System.Web.Services.WebService {

    public MyDocuments () {

        //Uncomment the following line if using designed components
        //InitializeComponent();
    }
```

```
        [WebMethod]
        public string HelloWorld() {
            return "Hello World";
        }

    }
```

The default code in the Web service has an initializing method called *MyDocuments* within the
MyDocuments class extending from System.Web.Services.WebServices. Several items are surrounded
by brackets. These are .NET attributes. Several are used before the *MyDocuments* class definition.
These define how the Web service will work. Attaching the *WebMethod* attribute to a *Public* method
indicates that you want the method exposed as part of the XML Web service. The *HelloWorld* method
is marked with this attribute. You can also use the properties of this attribute to further configure the
behavior of the XML Web service method.

You need to change the *WebService* temporary attribute for the Web service to work properly. Change
the *Namespace* value to **"http://VisualWebDeveloper.Chapter12"**. Your code should now look like
Listing 12-5.

LISTING 12 -5 MyDocuments.cs

```
using System;
using System.Collections.Generic;
using System.Linq;
using System.Web;
using System.Web.Services;


/// <summary>
/// Summary description for MyDocuments
/// </summary>
[WebService(Namespace = "http://VisualWebDeveloper.Chapter12")]
[WebServiceBinding(ConformsTo = WsiProfiles.BasicProfile1_1)]
// To allow this Web Service to be called from script, using ASP.NET AJAX, uncomment the
following line.
// [System.Web.Script.Services.ScriptService]
public class MyDocuments : System.Web.Services.WebService {

    public MyDocuments () {

        //Uncomment the following line if using designed components
        //InitializeComponent();
    }

    [WebMethod]
    public string HelloWorld() {
        return "Hello World";
    }

}
```

To run the Web service

1. Right-click MyDocuments.asmx in **Solution Explorer**. Select **Set As Start Page**.

    You need to do this to prevent the Login.aspx page from starting first.

2. Right-click **MyDocuments.asmx** in **Solution Explorer**. Select **View In Browser**. (See Figure 12-11.)

FIGURE 12-11 Running the Web service.

The browser opens to a Web page that displays the *HelloWorld* Web method. (See Figure 12-12.)

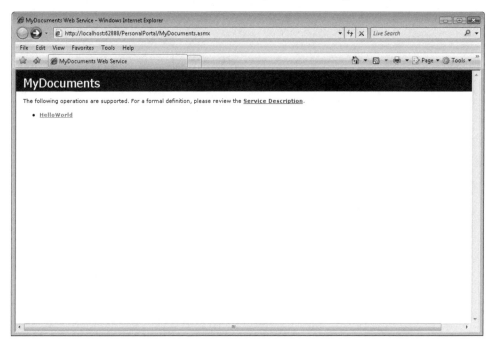

FIGURE 12-12 MyDocuments Web service operation list.

3. Click the **HelloWorld** link.

   A new Web page displays, enabling you to test the *HelloWorld* method. (See Figure 12-13.)

4. Click **Invoke**.

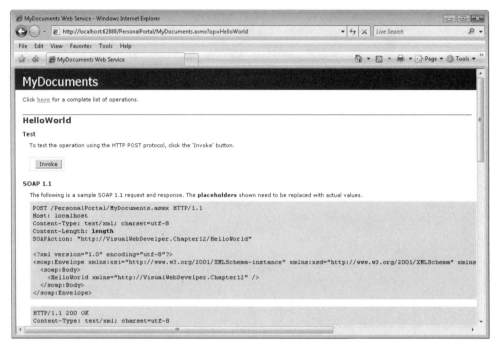

FIGURE 12-13 Web page to test *HelloWorld*.

5. Click **Invoke**.

The XML results are displayed in the browser. You can see the Hello World text within the *string* element. (See Figure 12-14.)

FIGURE 12-14 Results of the *HelloWorld* method.

Creating a Web Method

Now, create a custom method to retrieve the list of documents on the server. Rename the
HelloWorld method to **GetList()**. Type the code for *GetList* shown in Listing 12-6.

LISTING 12-6 THE *GETLIST* WEB METHOD

```
[WebMethod]
public string GetList() {

    string filenames = "";
    string[] files = System.IO.Directory.GetFiles(Server.MapPath("~/MyDocuments"),
"*.*");

    foreach (string s in files)
    {
        // Create the FileInfo object only when needed to ensure
        // the information is as current as possible.
        System.IO.FileInfo fi = null;
        try
        {
            fi = new System.IO.FileInfo(s);
        }
        catch (System.IO.FileNotFoundException e)
        {
            // To inform the user and continue is
```

```
            // sufficient for this demonstration.
            // Your application may require different behavior.
            Console.WriteLine(e.Message);
            continue;
        }
        filenames = filenames + fi.Name + ";";
    }

    return filenames;
}
```

The first two lines of code create a variable filename to hold the entire list of files that will be generated. The file's array of strings will hold the list of files returned by the *System. IO.Directory.GetFiles* method that uses the *Server.MapPath* method to get the path to the MyDocuments directory.

A foreach loop iterates through each string filename in the list and creates a new *System. IO.FileInfo* object to retrieve the filename without the path information. The *filenames* variable is concatenated with each filename and separated by a semicolon delimiter. This will be used by the code that calls the *GetList* function.

When you have added the code, it should look like Listing 12-7.

LISTING 12-7 *GetList* Web Method

```
using System;
using System.Collections.Generic;
using System.Linq;
using System.Web;
using System.Web.Services;


/// <summary>
/// Summary description for MyDocuments
/// </summary>
[WebService(Namespace = "http://VisualWebDeveloper.Chapter12")]
[WebServiceBinding(ConformsTo = WsiProfiles.BasicProfile1_1)]
// To allow this Web Service to be called from script, using ASP.NET AJAX, uncomment the
following line.
// [System.Web.Script.Services.ScriptService]
public class MyDocuments : System.Web.Services.WebService {

    public MyDocuments () {

        //Uncomment the following line if using designed components
        //InitializeComponent();

    }

    [WebMethod]
    public string GetList() {

        string filenames = "";
        string[] files = System.IO.Directory.GetFiles(Server.MapPath("~/MyDocuments"),
```

```
"*.*");

        foreach (string s in files)
        {
            // Create the FileInfo object only when needed to ensure
            // the information is as current as possible.
            System.IO.FileInfo fi = null;
            try
            {
                fi = new System.IO.FileInfo(s);
            }
            catch (System.IO.FileNotFoundException e)
            {
                // To inform the user and continue is
                // sufficient for this demonstration.
                // Your application may require different behavior.
                Console.WriteLine(e.Message);
                continue;
            }
            filenames = filenames + fi.Name + ";";
        }

        return filenames;
    }

}
```

Before you test the *GetList* Web method, remember to note the files that you have uploaded in the MyDocuments directory. In this example, I have two documents, Chapter 11.docx and Chapter 12.docx. (See Figure 12-15.)

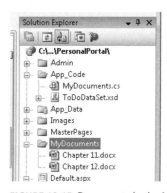

FIGURE 12-15 Documents in the MyDocuments folder.

Run the **MyDocuments** Web service as described earlier. The browser displays the *GetList* operation. Click the **GetList** operation link to show the Test Web page for it. (See Figure 12-16.)

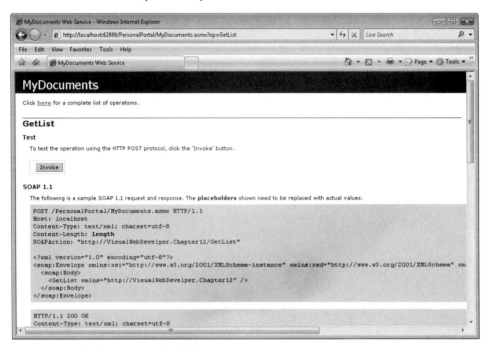

FIGURE 12-16 *GetList* operation Test Web page.

Click **Invoke**. The results of the *GetList* operation display in the browser. A list of the documents is displayed within XML, delimited by a semicolon: Chapter 11.docx;Chapter 12.docx;. (See Figure 12-17.)

FIGURE 12-17 Results of the *GetList* Web method.

Adding a Web Reference to a Project

You have created a Web service and a Web method to return the documents in your MyDocuments folder. Now you need to use it within the personal portal. Visual Web Developer enables you to reference Web services you create and make available externally. You can add a Web service to your project by creating a Web reference.

To create a Web reference

1. Right-click the personal portal project in **Solution Explorer**. Select **Add Web Reference**.

   The Add Web Reference dialog box displays. (See Figure 12-18.) There are three options to browse to: Web Services In This Solution, Web Services In This Local Machine, and Browse UDDI Servers On The Local Network.

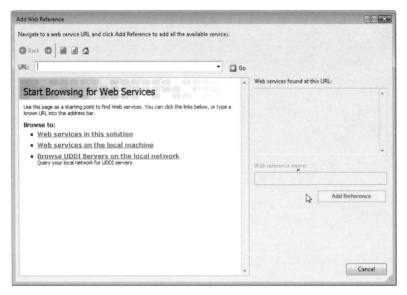

FIGURE 12-18 Add Web Reference dialog box.

2. Click **Web Services In The Solution**.

   The dialog box displays Web Services In This Solution: MyDocuments.

3. Click **MyDocuments**. (See Figure 12-19.)

FIGURE 12-19 MyDocuments Web service in the solution.

The Add Web Reference dialog box displays the URL for the MyDocuments Web service and the *GetList* Web method. (See Figure 12-20.)

4. Click the **Add Reference** button.

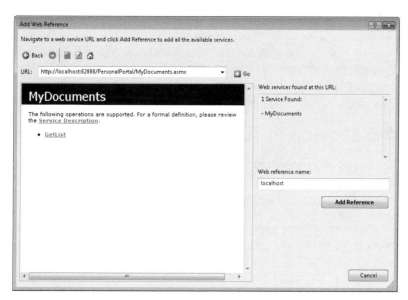

FIGURE 12-20 The *GetList* Web method.

A new folder, called App_WebReferences, is created in the project. Expanding the App_WebReferences and the localhost (the name of the Web reference) folders in Solution Explorer displays the Web references. (See Figure 12-21.)

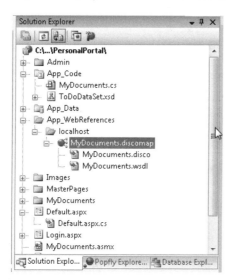

FIGURE 12-21 MyDocuments Web reference in Solution Explorer.

Two files constitute the Web reference: MyDocuments.disco and MyDocuments.wsdl.

Note DISCO is a Microsoft technology for publishing and discovering Web services. Universal Description, Discovery, and Integration (UDDI) is an industry-wide initiative that defines a SOAP-based protocol for updating and querying Web service information repositories. Like DISCO, UDDI makes it possible to publish and discover a Web service, maximizing the site's reach and ultimate success. You can read more about it at *http://msdn.microsoft.com/library/ms950421.aspx*.

Using a Web Service in ASP.NET

The Web service is integrated into the project and available to use. You will call the MyDocuments Web service and its *GetList* Web method. Using the MyDocuments Web service is no different than using any other object in C#.

Right-click the **Default.aspx** page in **Solution Explorer**. Select **View Markup**. Scroll down to the **Content** control for the **ContentPlaceholderId MyDocumentsContentPlaceholder**. The code should look like Listing 12-8.

LISTING 12-8 Content Control

```
<asp:Content ID="Content2" runat="server"
    contentplaceholderid="MyDocumentsContent">
    <asp:FileUpload ID="FileUpload1" runat="server" /><br />
    <asp:Button ID="BtnUpload" runat="server" Text="Upload"
        onclick="BtnUpload_Click" />
</asp:Content>
```

Below the button markup, add the following code in Listing 12-9.

LISTING 12-9 Code and Markup for Document List

```
<br/>Documents (Click on the document to download)
    <div style="background-color: White;">
    <%
        MyDocuments mydocs = new MyDocuments();
        string[] docList = mydocs.GetList().Split(';');
        for (int i = 0; i < docList.Length; i++)
        {
            Response.Write("<a href='MyDocuments/" + docList[i] + "'>" + docList[i] + "</
a><br/>");
        }
    %>
    </div>
```

The first line adds a line break and a label to direct the user to click the items in the list. You create a <div> with a white background color to hold the list of documents. Because you want to generate markup for the list of documents, you use inline ASP.NET that you used in Chapter 3. The MyDocuments Web service is created like you would create any object. A string list variable called *docList* will store the array of filenames returned from the Web service *GetList* method, and the *Split* string function is used to parse and separate the list of documents.

Using the *docList* string array, a for loop uses the *Response* object, as you did in Chapter 3, and its *Write* method is used to create markup dynamically for each document in the list. A hyperlink *<a>* element is created for each document with a *
* new line element.

To see how this works, click **Run** on the standard toolbar. The browser opens to the personal portal. Scroll down to the bottom of the page, to the **My Documents** section. (See Figure 12-22.)

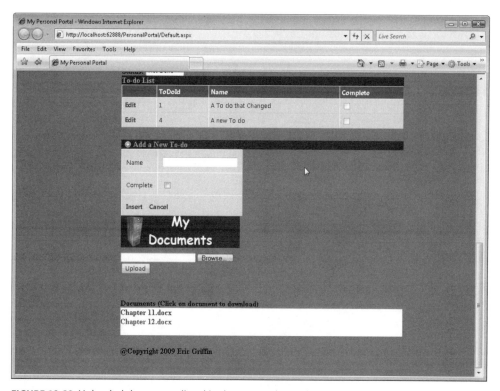

FIGURE 12-22 Uploaded documents listed in the personal portal.

Each document in the MyDocuments folder—in this case, Chapter 11.docx and Chapter 12.docx—is displayed in the list.

Click one of the documents to display the File Download dialog box. (See Figure 12-23.)

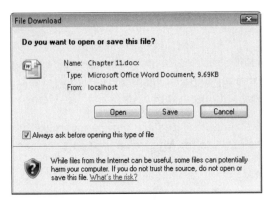

FIGURE 12-23 File download dialog box.

Summary

In this chapter, you learned about Web services. You learned how to upload documents to the server and how to create your own Web service, reference it in a project, and then use it in an ASP.NET page. In the next chapter, you will learn how to deploy your site to a remote location.

Chapter 13
Deploying Your Web Site

After completing this chapter, you will be able to

- Understand the factors involved with choosing a Web site hosting provider
- Install Internet Information Server 7 (IIS 7) on Windows Vista
- Create a new Web site on IIS 7
- Create a Web site ready to run ASP.NET pages
- Use Visual Web Developer to copy your Web site to a remote server

In Chapter 12, you learned how to use a vast array of features and ASP.NET technologies within Visual Web Developer. Along the way, you created a personal portal that can authenticate users, search maps, interact with a to-do database, view the news, and upload documents

This final chapter talks about deploying the personal portal by using Visual Web Developer. Fortunately, ASP.NET is supported by hosting service providers. These providers handle the hardware, software, and Internet connectivity required by any Web site. If you had to build this yourself, it could cost you thousands of dollars a month to maintain.

 Note You can find hundreds of Microsoft partners that provide hosted ASP.NET services on the Microsoft Web site at *http://microsoft.com/serviceproviders/directory/default.aspx*.

Shopping for a Provider

When you shop for an ASP.NET hosting provider, you need to consider several factors and weigh them against the number of ASP.NET pages and content, such as images, your personal portal will contain. Another factor to consider is the number of users you want to support on your site. The hosting price can be affected by the number of users who will access your site. The more there are, the higher the cost.

Cost

Monthly costs can be as low as $10 a month for small personal sites. These sites have just the basics: operating system, Web server, Internet connectivity and disk space to store your pages, and content. Many of the providers offer additional services such as e-mail, database, file transfer protocol sites (FTP), and ASP.NET controls that can be added at an incremental cost.

ASP.NET Support

.It's important for the provider to support the latest ASP.NET version. This should be ASP.NET 3.5 SP1. Many haven't upgraded from 2.0 yet, so this is an important feature to check.

Disk Space

This refers to the size of all the files within a Visual Web Developer project (that is, ASP.NET pages, style sheets, images, and so on). Typically, for small sites, 5 to 10 gigabytes (GB) is common and more than enough. If you are planning on uploading large images or files, you must consider that; it might raise the cost of your monthly service.

Domain Names

For your site to be found, it has to have a domain name, so if your site is to be called *http:// yourdomainhere.com*, you have to have it registered and assigned to the service provider. Most providers handle this and all the fees and maintenance of the domain name for you. This is great if you don't want the hassle of managing it yourself.

SQL Server Database Support

Many sites have database requirements. Support for Microsoft SQL Server is required by the personal portal, just as with many other sites.

Other Services

Many providers give you free ASP.NET controls as well as options to purchase and install other controls such as e-mail hosting for your domain (for instance, yourname@yourdomain. com) so you can send and receive e-mail. Statistics for your site is another popular service often offered for free. You can use the statistics to see who is visiting your site and when.

Creating Your Own Host

I am not going to recommend an ASP.NET host provider in this book. There are many to choose from, and it needs to be your choice, based on some of the criteria I listed, which one is best for you.

You can simulate the process of using a host by setting up a Web server on your own computer. The instructions in this chapter are for Windows Vista Home edition, Windows Vista Business edition, or Window Vista Ultimate. These operating systems enable you to set up your own Web server and host a Web site from your computer. The Windows Vista built-in Web server is called Internet Information Server (IIS).

The first thing to do is install Internet Information Server. The following steps are for Windows Vista Home edition, Windows Vista Business edition, or Window Vista Ultimate edition.

To install Internet Information Server

1. Open **Control Panel** from the **Start** menu. Click **Programs**. (See Figure 13-1.)

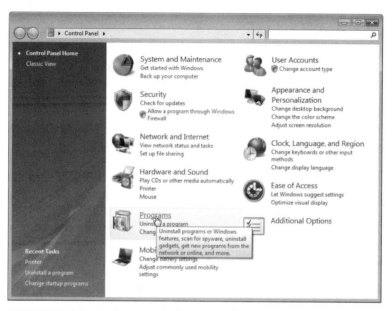

FIGURE 13-1 Selecting Programs in Control Panel.

2. In **Programs And Features**, select **Turn Windows Features On Or Off**. (See Figure 13-2.)

FIGURE 13-2 Selecting Turn Windows Features On Or Off.

The Windows Features dialog box appears.

3. Scroll down and expand **Internet Information Services** to display three more nodes: FTP Publishing Service, Web Management Tools, and World Wide Web Services. (See Figure 13-3.)

FIGURE 13-3 Viewing Internet Information Services features.

4. Expand **Web Management Tools** and select **IIS 6 Management Compatibility** and **IIS Management Console**. (See Figure 13-4.)

FIGURE 13-4 Selecting the Web Management tools.

5. Expand **World Wide Web Services** and **Application Development Features**. Select **ASP.NET**. Leave any selected default features. (In Figure 13-5, CGI is selected by default.)

   The .NET Extensibility, ISAPI Extensions, and Filters check boxes automatically are selected.

FIGURE 13-5 Enabling ASP.NET.

An installation dialog box appears. (See Figure 13-6.) It might take several minutes while Windows Vista configures itself.

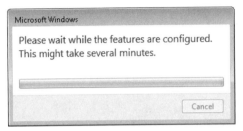

FIGURE 13-6 Installation dialog box.

Note If you receive the "An Error Has Occurred. Not All Features Were Successfully Changed" error, please refer to Microsoft Knowledgebase article 929772. Follow the steps to resolve the issue at *http://support.microsoft.com/kb/929772*.

The installation dialog box disappears.

6. Open Microsoft Internet Explorer and navigate to *http://localhost*. The IIS 7 Web page appears. (See Figure 13-7.)

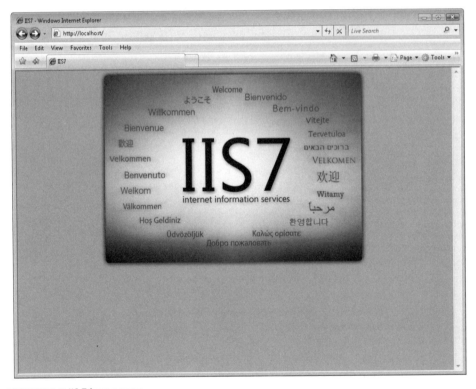

FIGURE 13-7 IIS 7 home page.

Creating the Personal Portal Web Site

IIS 7 has been installed, but what has changed? The first important thing to understand is where the Web site files will reside on your computer. When IIS 7 is installed, it creates a folder called Inetpub. This directory is always on the root drive (that is, C:\inetpub). A subdirectory under it, called wwwroot, contains all directories that are related to a Web site. (See Figure 13-8.) The first thing to do is create a directory under wwwroot for the personal portal.

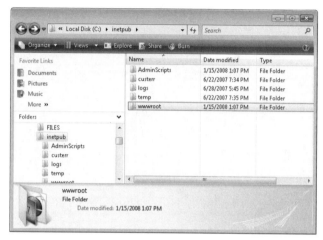

FIGURE 13-8 Root site for all Web sites.

To create a Web site in IIS 7

1. Create a new folder and name it **personalportal**.

2. From the **Start** menu, type **inetmgr** in the search bar. Click the program that appears at the top of the list.

   The Internet Information Services Manager appears.

3. Expand the top-level node, which should be the name of your computer. Expand **Web Sites** and then **Default Web Site**.

   You should see the personalportal folder you created. (See Figure 13-9.)

FIGURE 13-9 The personalportal folder.

Right now, any HTML files can be served from that directory by typing, for example, **http://localhost/personalportal/nameofpage.html**. However, ASP.NET pages require the site to be converted into an IIS 7 application.

4. Right-click the **personalportal** folder. Select **Convert to Application**. (See Figure 13-10.)

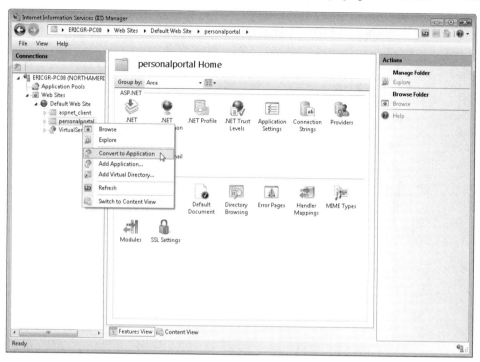

FIGURE 13-10 Converting personalportal to an application.

The Add Application dialog box appears. Make no changes.

5. Click **OK**. (See Figure 13-11.)

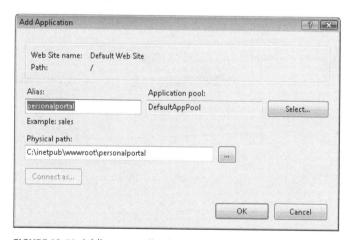

FIGURE 13-11 Adding an application to the server.

In Chapter 3, you created your first ASP.NET pages.

6. Retrieve **default.aspx** from the Chapter 3 code folder on this book's companion CD. Copy it to the **personalportal** folder. Rename the file **Default.aspx**.

7. Return to **Internet Information Server Manager**. Right-click the **personalportal** application and select **Refresh**.

You will see Default.aspx and Web.config. This was created by default for the new personalportal application. (See Figure 13-12.)

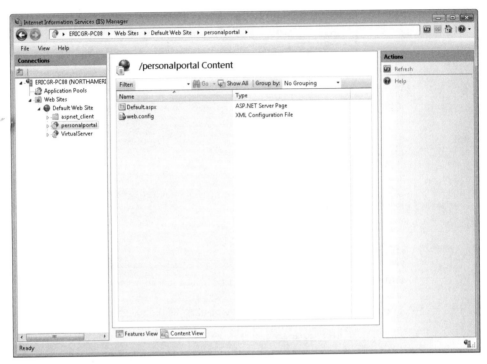

FIGURE 13-12 Personal portal with the Default.aspx page.

8. Right-click the **personalportal** application and select **Browse**.

The browser opens, displaying the Default.aspx page from Chapter 3. (See Figure 13-13.)

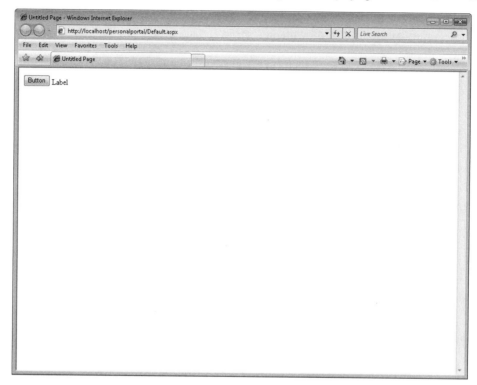

FIGURE 13-13 Default.aspx page running.

Copying a Web Site with Visual Web Developer

You have installed a Web server, created a new site, and made sure that it can serve ASP.NET pages. Now you can use Visual Web Developer to copy the site to the server. There are four ways to copy a site: File System, Local IIS, FTP Site, and Remote Web Site.

- **File System**   This is similar to the manual copying and pasting you did with the Chapter 3 .aspx page.

- **Local IIS**   This enables you, when you run Visual Web Developer as administrator, to copy your project by using Web protocols.

- **FTP Site**   Many hosting service providers allow you to upload your files to the Web server directory by using FTP

- **Remote Web Site**   This requires Microsoft FrontPage server extensions to be installed and enabled on the server. Windows Vista does not support FrontPage server extensions.

Let's walk through the Local IIS option because Windows Vista does not support FrontPage server extensions used by the Remote Web Site option. The interface is similar for each option.

To copy the Web site to the server, using the Local IIS option

1. Right-click the **Visual Web Developer** icon and select **Run As Administrator**.

2. Open the **personalportal** project. Select **Copy Web Site**. (See Figure 13-14.)

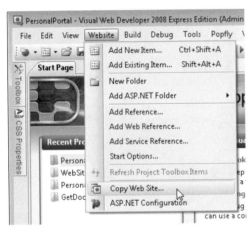

FIGURE 13-14 Copy Web Site menu item.

The Copy Web Site page appears. (See Figure 13-15.)

3. Click **Connect**.

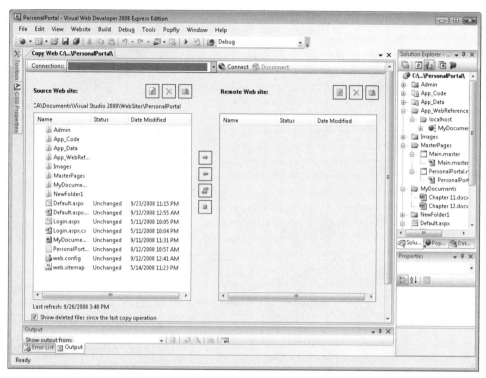

FIGURE 13-15 Copy Web Site page.

The Open Web site dialog box appears.

4. Select **Local IIS**, to the right of the dialog box.

   The local Web servers display in the list.

5. Expand the **Default Web Site** node and select the **personalportal** application. (See Figure 13-16.) Click **Open**.

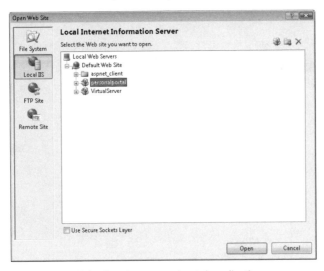

FIGURE 13-16 Selecting the personalportal application.

The personal portal Web site directory displays on the left list. The Web Server personal portal list to the right is empty. (See Figure 13-17.)

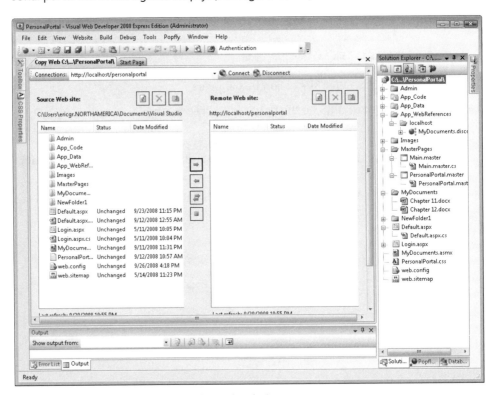

FIGURE 13-17 Connected to the personal portal Web site.

6. Select all the files and folders in the **Source Web Site** list. Click the top button with the arrow pointing to the personal portal Web site on the right.

The site is copied to the Web server. (See Figure 13-18.) Note that there are arrow buttons that represent copying the files to the project Web site and synchronizing between the two sites.

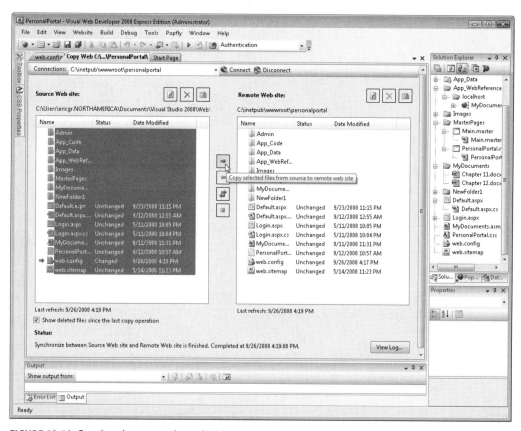

FIGURE 13-18 Copying the personalportal Web site.

7. Return to **Internet Information Services Manager** and right-click the **personalportal** application. Select **Browse**. (See Figure 13-19.)

FIGURE 13-19 Browsing the personal portal.

The browser opens, and the personal portal appears, running from your local host Web server. (See Figure 13-20.)

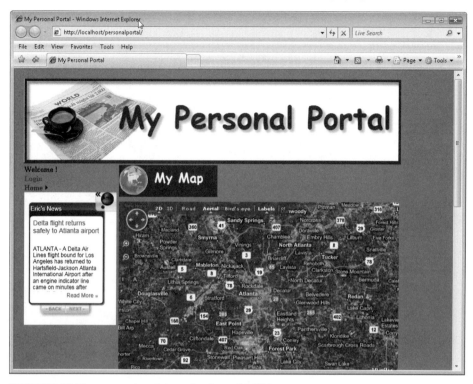

FIGURE 13-20 The personal portal running from the Web server.

Summary

In this final chapter, you explored how you can transfer your personal portal project to a remote Web server. You simulated this by installing a Web server called Microsoft Internet Information Server, which comes built into Windows Vista, on your computer. You used the Copy Web Site feature in Visual Web Developer to transfer the entire site with a button click.

Index

For Web Developers

**Microsoft® ASP.NET 3.5
Step by Step**

George Shepherd

ISBN 9780735624269

Teach yourself ASP.NET 3.5—one step at a time. Ideal for developers with fundamental programming skills but new to ASP.NET, this practical tutorial delivers hands-on guidance for developing Web applications in the Microsoft Visual Studio® 2008 environment.

**Microsoft Visual Web
Developer 2008
Express Edition
Step by Step**

Eric Griffin

ISBN 9780735626065

Your hands guide to learning fundamental Web-development skills. This tutorial steps you through an end-to-end example, helping build essential skills logically and sequentially. By the end of the book, you'll have a working Web site, plus the fundamental skills needed for the next level—ASP.NET.

**Introducing Microsoft
Silverlight™ 2,**
Second Edition

Laurence Moroney

ISBN 9780735625280

Get a head start with Silverlight 2—the cross-platform, cross-browser plug-in for rich interactive applications and the next-generation user experience. Featuring advance insights from inside the Silverlight team, this book delivers the practical, approachable guidance and code to inspire your next solutions.

**Programming Microsoft
ASP.NET 3.5**

Dino Esposito

ISBN 9780735625273

The definitive guide to ASP.NET 3.5. Led by well-known ASP.NET expert Dino Esposito, you'll delve into the core topics for creating innovative Web applications, including Dynamic Data; LINQ; state, application, and session management; Web forms and requests; security strategies; AJAX; Silverlight; and more.

**JavaScript
Step by Step**

Steve Suehring

ISBN 9780735624498

Build on your fundamental programming skills, and get hands-on guidance for creating Web applications with JavaScript. Learn to work with the six JavaScript data types, the Document Object Model, Web forms, CSS styles, AJAX, and other essentials—one step at a time.

Programming Microsoft LINQ

Paolo Pialorsi and Marco Russo

ISBN 9780735624009

With LINQ, you can query data—no matter what the source—directly from Microsoft Visual Basic® or C#. Guided by two data-access experts who've worked with LINQ in depth, you'll learn how Microsoft .NET Framework 3.5 implements LINQ, and how to exploit it. Study and adapt the book's examples for faster, leaner code.

ALSO SEE

**Developing Service-Oriented AJAX
Applications on the Microsoft Platform**
ISBN 9780735625914

Microsoft ASP.NET 2.0 Step by Step
ISBN 9780735622012

Programming Microsoft ASP.NET 2.0
ISBN 9780735625273

**Programming Microsoft ASP.NET 2.0
Applications: Advanced Topics**
ISBN 9780735621770

Collaborative Technologies— Resources for Developers

Inside Microsoft® Windows® SharePoint® Services 3.0
Ted Pattison, Daniel Larson
ISBN 9780735623200

Get the in-depth architectural insights, task-oriented guidance, and extensive code samples you need to build robust, enterprise content-management solutions.

Inside Microsoft Office SharePoint Server 2007
Patrick Tisseghem
ISBN 9780735623682

Led by an expert in collaboration technologies, you'll plumb the internals of SharePoint Server 2007—and master the intricacies of developing intranets, extranets, and Web-based applications.

Inside the Index and Search Engines: Microsoft Office SharePoint Server 2007
Patrick Tisseghem, Lars Fastrup
ISBN 9780735625358

Customize and extend the enterprise search capabilities in SharePoint Server 2007—and optimize the user experience—with guidance from two recognized SharePoint experts.

Working with Microsoft Dynamics® CRM 4.0, Second Edition
Mike Snyder, Jim Steger
ISBN 9780735623781

Whether you're an IT professional, a developer, or a power user, get real-world guidance on how to make Microsoft Dynamics CRM work the way you do—with or without programming.

Programming Microsoft Dynamics CRM 4.0
Jim Steger et al.
ISBN 9780735625945

Apply the design and coding practices that leading CRM consultants use to customize, integrate, and extend Microsoft Dynamics CRM 4.0 for specific business needs.

ALSO SEE

Inside Microsoft Dynamics AX 2009
ISBN 9780735626454

6 Microsoft Office Business Applications for Office SharePoint Server 2007
ISBN 9780735622760

Programming Microsoft Office Business Applications
ISBN 9780735625365

Inside Microsoft Exchange Server 2007 Web Services
ISBN 9780735623927

Microsoft®
Press

microsoft.com/mspress

For C# Developers

Microsoft® Visual C#® 2008 Express Edition: Build a Program Now!

Patrice Pelland

ISBN 9780735625426

Build your own Web browser or other cool application—no programming experience required! Featuring learn-by-doing projects and plenty of examples, this full-color guide is your quick start to creating your first applications for Windows®. DVD includes Express Edition software plus code samples.

Learn Programming Now! Microsoft XNA® Game Studio 2.0

Rob Miles

ISBN 9780735625228

Now you can create your own games for Xbox 360® and Windows—as you learn the underlying skills and concepts for computer programming. Dive right into your first project, adding new tools and tricks to your arsenal as you go. Master the fundamentals of XNA Game Studio and Visual C#—no experience required!

Windows via C/C++, Fifth Edition

Jeffrey Richter, Christophe Nasarre

ISBN 9780735624245

Jeffrey Richter's classic guide to C++ programming—now fully revised for Windows XP, Windows Vista®, and Windows Server® 2008. Learn to develop more-robust applications with unmanaged C++ code—and apply advanced techniques—with comprehensive guidance and code samples from the experts.

Microsoft Visual C# 2008 Step by Step

John Sharp

ISBN 9780735624306

Teach yourself Visual C# 2008—one step at a time. Ideal for developers with fundamental programming skills, this practical tutorial delivers hands-on guidance for creating C# components and Windows–based applications. CD features practice exercises, code samples, and a fully searchable eBook.

Programming Microsoft Visual C# 2008: The Language

Donis Marshall

ISBN 9780735625402

Get the in-depth reference, best practices, and code you need to master the core language capabilities in Visual C# 2008. Fully updated for Microsoft .NET Framework 3.5, including a detailed exploration of LINQ, this book examines language features in detail—and across the product life cycle.

CLR via C#, Second Edition

Jeffrey Richter

ISBN 9780735621633

Dig deep and master the intricacies of the common language runtime (CLR) and the .NET Framework. Written by programming expert Jeffrey Richter, this guide is ideal for developers building any kind of application—ASP.NET, Windows Forms, Microsoft SQL Server®, Web services, console apps—and features extensive C# code samples.

ALSO SEE

Microsoft Visual C# 2005 Step by Step
ISBN 9780735621299

Programming Microsoft Visual C# 2005: The Language
ISBN 9780735621817

Debugging Microsoft .NET 2.0 Applications
ISBN 9780735622029

Best Practices for Software Engineering

Software Estimation: Demystifying the Black Art
Steve McConnell
ISBN 9780735605350

Amazon.com's pick for "Best Computer Book of 2006"! Generating accurate software estimates is fairly straightforward—once you understand the art of creating them. Acclaimed author Steve McConnell demystifies the process—illuminating the practical procedures, formulas, and heuristics you can apply right away.

Code Complete, Second Edition
Steve McConnell
ISBN 9780735619678

Widely considered one of the best practical guides to programming—fully updated. Drawing from research, academia, and everyday commercial practice, McConnell synthesizes must-know principles and techniques into clear, pragmatic guidance. Rethink your approach—and deliver the highest quality code.

Agile Portfolio Management
Jochen Krebs
ISBN 9780735625679

Agile processes foster better collaboration, innovation, and results. So why limit their use to software projects—when you can transform your entire business? This book illuminates the opportunities—and rewards—of applying agile processes to your overall IT portfolio, with best practices for optimizing results.

Simple Architectures for Complex Enterprises
Roger Sessions
ISBN 9780735625785

Why do so many IT projects fail? Enterprise consultant Roger Sessions believes complex problems require simple solutions. And in this book, he shows how to make simplicity a core architectural requirement—as critical as performance, reliability, or security—to achieve better, more reliable results for your organization.

The Enterprise and Scrum
Ken Schwaber
ISBN 9780735623378

Extend Scrum's benefits—greater agility, higher-quality products, and lower costs—beyond individual teams to the entire enterprise. Scrum cofounder Ken Schwaber describes proven practices for adopting Scrum principles across your organization, including that all-critical component—managing change.

ALSO SEE

Software Requirements, Second Edition
Karl E. Wiegers
ISBN 9780735618794

More About Software Requirements: Thorny Issues and Practical Advice
Karl E. Wiegers
ISBN 9780735622678

Software Requirement Patterns
Stephen Withall
ISBN 9780735623989

Agile Project Management with Scrum
Ken Schwaber
ISBN 9780735619937

For Visual Basic Developers

Microsoft® Visual Basic® 2008 Express Edition: Build a Program Now!

Patrice Pelland

ISBN 9780735625419

Build your own Web browser or other cool application—no programming experience required! Featuring learn-by-doing projects and plenty of examples, this full-color guide is your quick start to creating your first applications for Windows®. DVD includes Express Edition software plus code samples.

Microsoft Visual Basic 2008 Step by Step

Michael Halvorson

ISBN 9780735625372

Teach yourself the essential tools and techniques for Visual Basic 2008—one step at a time. No matter what your skill level, you'll find the practical guidance and examples you need to start building applications for Windows and the Web. CD features practice exercises, code samples, and a fully searchable eBook.

Programming Microsoft Visual Basic 2005: The Language

Francesco Balena

ISBN 9780735621831

Master the core capabilities in Visual Basic 2005 with guidance from well-known programming expert Francesco Balena. Focusing on language features and the Microsoft .NET Framework 2.0 base class library, this book provides pragmatic instruction and examples useful to both new and experienced developers.

Programming Windows Services with Microsoft Visual Basic 2008

Michael Gernaey

ISBN 9780735624337

The essential guide for developing powerful, customized Windows services with Visual Basic 2008. Whether you're looking to perform network monitoring or design a complex enterprise solution, this guide delivers the right combination of expert advice and practical examples to accelerate your productivity.

ALSO SEE

Microsoft Visual Basic 2005 Express Edition: Build a Program Now!
Patrice Pelland
ISBN 9780735622135

Microsoft Visual Basic 2005 Step by Step
Michael Halvorson
ISBN 9780735621312

Microsoft ADO.NET 2.0 Step by Step
Rebecca Riordan
ISBN 9780735621640

Microsoft ASP.NET 3.5 Step by Step
George Shepherd
ISBN 9780735624269

Programming Microsoft ASP.NET 3.5
Dino Esposito
ISBN 9780735625273

Debugging Microsoft .NET 2.0 Applications
John Robbins
ISBN 9780735622029

***Microsoft*®**
Press

microsoft.com/mspress

Eric Griffin

Eric Griffin works at Microsoft as a Senior Technical Strategy Advisor, where he aligns Microsoft innovations with products from a portfolio of strategic partners. In his 18-year career, Eric has led and mentored developers, created commercial applications, and published articles in *MSDN* magazine and Wrox's *ASP Today*. His book *Foundations of Popfly* was recently published by Apress. He is studying Management and Leadership, Strategy and Innovation at the MIT Sloan School of Management. An occasional science fiction writer, Eric was the winner of the 2003 Phobos Books Fiction Contest. A resident of Atlanta, Georgia, Eric and his wife, Susan, have five children.

What do you think of this book?

We want to hear from you!

Do you have a few minutes to participate in a brief online survey?

Microsoft is interested in hearing your feedback so we can continually improve our books and learning resources for you.

To participate in our survey, please visit:

www.microsoft.com/learning/booksurvey/

...and enter this book's ISBN-10 or ISBN-13 number (located above barcode on back cover*). As a thank-you to survey participants in the United States and Canada, each month we'll randomly select five respondents to win one of five $100 gift certificates from a leading online merchant. At the conclusion of the survey, you can enter the drawing by providing your e-mail address, which will be used for prize notification only.

Thanks in advance for your input. Your opinion counts!

* Where to find the ISBN on back cover

ISBN-13: 000-0-0000-0000-0
ISBN-10: 0-0000-0000-0

0 000000 000000

Example only. Each book has unique ISBN.

Microsoft®
Press